DARE to DREAM

HEALING FEARS, CREATING MIRACLES, & LIVING YOUR DREAMS

MARGARET ALLEN HILLER
AND DAVID HILLER

HEART DREAM PRESS

Published by Heart Dream Press
238 N. Wightman St.
Ashland, Or. 97520

miracles1@mindspring.com

Cover & Interior Design by Lightbourne

ISBN: 0-9720120-0-1
Library of Congress Control Number: 2002107104

Printed in the United States of America
10 9 8 7 6 5 4 3 2 1

CONTENTS

ACKNOWLEDGMENTS

In gratitude,

D*are to Dream* is one of our dreams come true. We are so grateful for all those who held the vision and supported us in the creation of this book. We would like to say Thank you for your loving thoughts, creative ideas, and wonderful support to: Danese Allen; Jonah Anderson; Robert Arnott; Mike Beasley; Alberta Boccaleoni; Pat Crowe; Diane Doiron; Mel, Sam, and Nate Engles; Tore Gintoli; Fran and Jim Hurlbut; Maryellen Kelley; Dr. Ben Keyes; Dhyana Kuta; Shoshanna Love; Alyssa Lukara; Betty Luna; Deborah McCoy; Tina Pomroy; Drayton Riley; Michael Roberts; Katar and Darryl Schoenstadt; Mary Staton; Dr. Margaret Stevens; Mary Kacey Taylor; Barbara Thomas; Calvin and Dr. Darlene Walsh-Martin; Doug and Penny Werth; Phyllis and Pete Weis; Carl and Johanna Wright; Margo and Brian Young; and Te Zins.

Thanks to Margaret's family: Lillian and Grady Allen (Mom and Dad); and her sisters, Pam Allen and Joan Swanson, for their love and valuable support.

Thanks to David's Mom, Betty Hiller; his sister, Barb, and brother, Rick, for all their love and support.

A special acknowledgment to David's daughter, Tanya Hiller, for being a most exceptional dream come true in David's life.

We want to give special thanks to Shannon and Gaelyn at Lightbourne in Ashland, Oregon, for their design of the book interior and cover, and for their exceptional creativity and encouragement.

Thanks to Shanti Einolander for her help with the final edits, and for embracing both us and the book so tenderly; and to Julia Tucker for being with us from the beginning of the project with her unceasing, energetic support and encouragement, cheering us on, and doing whatever it took to keep us "on track" with her editing and our writing schedules.

To Gypsy, our beloved wolf-husky, for being there for us with unconditional love every step of the way since the three of us started our journey together in 1992.

Finally, our thanks to Great Spirit for blessing us in our lives and in our work, and for the inspiration of writing this book together. And thanks to each other for Daring to dream the holy dream for our lives, our marriage, our work, and for bringing our book into the world—a dream come true.

INTRODUCTION

Henry David Thoreau believed that if we advance confidently in the direction of our dreams and endeavor to live the life we have imagined, we will meet with extraordinary success, pass invisible boundaries, and be surrounded by new universal laws and a higher order of being. *Dare to Dream* is about dreaming the holiest dreams for our lives, our children, our community, our country, and the world. It is about "advancing confidently in the direction" of creating those dreams.

The theme of the book originally came to David during one of his sleeping dreams. From this dream, we created seminars and workshops on dreaming holy dreams rather than dreams of fear.

A few weeks after September 11th, 2001, we were reflecting and praying about world events when we both received the same inspiration to create a book on the theme, "Dare to Dream." As you can see, we absolutely believe that sleeping dreams are a vital and viable part of guidance and connection to Spirit. Each one of us must give attention to the "All of It," meaning, all the ways Spirit guides us, through sleeping dreams, waking dreams, ponderings, reflections, inspired ideas, prayer, meditation, and every life experience.

Dare to Dream emphasizes the importance of our *awake dreaming*—holding holy vision and manifesting our dreams.

Our book is a collection of stories and teachings with guided practices to enable you to live consciously and create your dreams. Much of our own personal journeys are in the stories. Most of all, Spirit is in the stories. We have witnessed many miracles throughout the world over the last twenty years and have personally created some very special dreams for ourselves, as well as supporting others in creating dreams by serving on their "vision teams." The stories encourage all of us to release fears, to heal, to dream holy dreams, to envision remarkable outcomes, to create miracles, and to live as if our presence in the world really makes a difference—because it does!

Each chapter ends with a "Dare to Dream" process to support you in the practice of living a richer, fuller, happier life. We have also included a thirty-day coaching plan that you can use as a guide to take action and live your dreams.

As counselors, teachers, and healers, we have witnessed the resiliency and the deep spiritual and emotional strength of human beings who dare to dream and create remarkable outcomes for themselves, their families, and others. We have noticed an exceptional increase in the degree of commitment in the hearts of many people who want to make a positive difference in the world, especially since September 11th. We believe that all of us have received an emergency call from the Divine to be holy visionaries, and there is much evidence to indicate that the call is being answered. We are seeing a "metanoia," a "change of heart" for humankind, leading to a greater consciousness of love, compassion, and right action toward all of life.

We hold this holy vision, prayer, and dream for you: May you remember yourself as an eternal spiritual being. May you know that Spirit lives within and around you. May you feel Spirit enlivening your body, invigorating your mind, and increasing your awareness that your holy dreams are needed in the world. May you know that your presence makes a difference and that your thoughts, words, and actions can create healing. May you Dare to Dream the Holiest Dream that blesses you, all those you hold dearly in your heart, and the world.

DREAMING THE HOLIEST DREAM

Believe it! It's real. Dreams do come true! Know in your heart that all things are possible and set your dreams free. Life's ever-unfolding magnificent dream lives within us. It is evolving and pulsating in every atom and cell. Two thousand years ago, The Christ said, "The Kingdom of Heaven is within you." Twelve hundred years later, Rumi, the 13th century Persian teacher and poet, said "We have placed in you a substance, a seeking, a yearning. We are watching over it and won't let it be lost, but will bring it to its destined place."

Currently in the new millennium, many of us know in our hearts that the "substance" Rumi spoke of and the "Kingdom of Heaven" are one and the same. It is the enlivening presence of Spirit within us—God, Divine Mind, the Great Mystery that created all the Universes—those that we can see and those yet to be seen.

The evolution of God consciousness is more apparent than ever before. Humankind is awakening to Holy Dream, the creation of Heaven on Earth through love, compassion, and right action toward all beings, all of life, in the air, the water, the planet itself, and humankind. Ultimately, our individual dreams work together with God's Great Dream for us, to know that the Kingdom of Heaven lives within our hearts. Whether we're dreaming for children to be safe, our Earth to be protected, a way to build hospitals and schools in impoverished countries, or for well being in our personal lives, Holy Dream is awakening within us and creating through us.

Holy is defined by *The New World Dictionary* as "whole, happy, belonging to or coming from God, sacred, and regarded with or deserving deep respect, awe, reverence or adoration." These are not only definitions of Holy Dream but also concepts that each of us are learning to apply to ourselves and others. How can we believe in and create our dreams if we do not believe in ourselves and know who we truly are?

Rumi asks, "Who are you? What is your real name?" We are the eternal presence of God expressing in the form of human beings. With all of humankind's varied thoughts, feelings, emotions, beliefs and actions, we are expressions of God and are created and coded with the potential for wholeness, kindness, happiness, and deserving of respect, awe, reverence, and adoration.

In our work as counselors and healers, David and I occasionally see people who have lost hope, forgotten the importance of their dreams, or feel blocked in connecting with or moving forward in those dreams. Some no longer dare to dream at all. We hear individuals say things like, "I don't know what my dreams are," or, "I don't know my life purpose or what I'm supposed to be doing with my life." Those feelings and beliefs keep us from being inspired, which is the energy needed to birth Holy Dream.

When David hears these kinds of statements, he asks a "trick" question: "If you *did* know your dream or life purpose, what would it be?" At that point, they often look a bit baffled, then smile, and quickly shift into the imagination of their heart. "Well," they say, "if I *did* know what my dream was, then it would be . . ." Amazing how effective the imagination is!

Sometimes it's as simple as that, just asking the right question of our true self—the heart, soul, or creative mind. Then allowing the answers to come. It is written in scripture that God said, "I could not bless my people because they would not ask." It is essential to know what our dreams are in order to create them. Asking, praying, and envisioning are all components of getting to our dreams. Paying attention to both the night dreams and the day dreams, and imagining our lives unfolding in healthy ways, are all a part of creating and allowing Holy Dream to manifest in our lives. This, in turn, projects hope for a better world.

In the film *The Wizard of Oz,* Judy Garland sings ". . . and the dreams that you dare to dream really do come true." In the song these dreams are "somewhere over the rainbow," a symbol of promise in a land of hope. It is the land of the heart where great potential, hope, and creative dream consciousness live. Healers, visionaries, and dreamers listen to their hearts for inspired ideas and messages and dare to dream great possibilities.

Are you imagining and envisioning for healing, peace, and well being in your life? What about for your beloveds and for the world? If so, you are a presence of healing in the world, a presence of life-renewing energy for all those you touch with your thoughts, words, and actions. You are a healer. If you doubt this, take this survey:

1. Do you have a heart? (We'll pause here while you check!)

2. Do you smile, weep, or feel compassion for self, and do you connect with others in this way?

3. Do you say a kind word to yourself or someone else who also needs encouragement?

4. Are you present with your eyes, your hands, a hug, or an action toward someone who is afraid or lonely and needs human contact?

If you answered yes to these questions, then guess what? You're out of the closet! You're a healer. Love is what heals! The more people who realize this, the more healing consciousness will emerge and expand in our world.

There are all kinds of healers on the planet, and they live in many forms, some of which are called by these names: Children, Angels, Four-Leggeds, Winged Ones, Sisters, Flowers, Trees, Curanderas, Shamans, Ministers, Mothers, Therapists, Doctors, Fathers, Teachers, Friends, Grandfathers, Counselors, Dancers, Grandmothers, Writers, Gardeners, Builders, Hair Dressers, Brothers, Musicians, Beekeepers . . . and on, and on.

Visionaries and Healers have the same qualities of caring, concern, and compassion for self and others. They dream for the world to be a place of peace and kindness. They know that their thoughts, words, actions, and presence can make a life-giving rather than life-depleting difference in the world. In his book, *Making Miracles*,[1] Paul Pearsall outlined four important aspects of healers and visionaries who create remarkable outcomes. When individuals envision healing and create dreams with miracle consciousness, they:

1. Maintain a perception of hope. No matter what the

situation looks like, they view it through the eyes of hope.

2. See chaos as an opportunity for healing. As the quantum physicists tell us, chaos is required to create the new form. An example of this is seen in time-lapse photography of a zygote when it starts to divide. There appears to be a lot of shaking and chaos happening in this process, yet cell division is the basic beginning of all life. In life and in dreams there is sometimes a "division." It feels like a break-ing down or shaking up of things, a sign that there is a new form yearning to be revealed and created.

3. Look for signs of serendipity, connection, and syn-chronicity at all times. Watch for doors to open or close, the arrival of people, information, or resources as they are needed, and for Life/Universe to bring all that is required for creation of the dream.

4. Have loving kindness for self and others.

Notice that self is listed first here. It's not the way most of us were taught, is it? We cannot truly show love or kind-ness to others unless we are first loving, kind, and caring to ourselves.

Apply these "Miracle Rules" to how you hold your dream, how you look upon your dream and see life energy moving around it. Are you caring for it, kindly attending to it, seeing it with eyes of hope, even during chaos? Are you watching for the connecting pieces to show up at the perfect time? Are you celebrating your dream and giving thanks for its presence living in you?

When the Navajo pray for rain, they come together and

give thanks for the rain and celebrate its arrival before they ever see the first raindrop. It is always good to gather with others who believe in you and your dreams and to celebrate before you ever see them literally created.

One of the great things about living in this day and time is learning about the importance and value of support groups. Mastermind groups, creativity groups, brainstorming groups, and prayer groups are all helpful in getting clear on your dreams, moving forward, taking action, and manifesting them.

David and I like to work with Vision Teams. Our visionaries are spread out all over the country and other parts of the world. They are individuals whom we respect, who know and value us and the dreams we hold in our hearts. We can call or e-mail them and say, "Please hold the vision with us," meaning, "Pray with us and see God at work with us," for a particular project, healing, or idea to unfold so that we are in alignment with creating the perfect outcome for ourselves and our lives.

For example, when David and I clearly "got it," after a lot of prayer and listening and reflection, that we wanted to write *Dare to Dream*, we called together a group of people to hold the vision with us. We gave them permission to ask us questions and give us feedback to help us clarify the dream. We asked them to know and envision with us that we would be inspired, disciplined, and guided in every step of the process; that we would write a book that would inspire and support others to heal fears, create miracles, and live their dreams. We not only asked these "teammates" to pray and hold the vision with us, we also asked them to say words of encouragement to "lift us in spirit," to help boost and launch us into the dream energy more than we could by ourselves.

An important career position that provides lots of support and encouragement and is becoming more popular and appreciated in the world right now is the "doula." Defined in the Greek language as "mothering the mother," the doula is not a midwife, but rather a coach who provides emotional support with the objective of helping the mother make healthy decisions. She supports the mother with nurturing energy and helps to protect and create a holy memory of the birth experience (See Doulas of North America website at www.dona.com). Research shows that having a doula on the birth team creates these impressive results:

25% shorter labor
50% fewer cesareans
60% reduction in epidurals
40% less usage of forceps
30% reduction in pain medications
Improved breastfeeding
Greater maternal feelings and enhanced bonding
Decreased postpartum depression

Having a supportive individual or a group vision team is like having your own doula. They know with you that your dream is possible and that you have everything you need and require to take each step of the journey toward fulfilling your dream. If there are moments of feeling lost or not knowing what the next step is, receiving a phone call or visit from someone on your vision team is a great opportunity to be "coached" into action. You may hear things like, "Please don't quit. You can do this. I'm holding the vision with you. Keep breathing." They're your coaches in birthing your dream and can help reduce the labor or pain, if there is any. They can help you "bond" with your dream if it feels elusive to you.

The Hopi Nation in Oraibi, Arizona gives us this important message entitled "Wisdom of the Elders":

There is a river flowing now very fast. It is so great and swift that there are those who will be afraid. They will try to hold on to the shore. They will feel they are being torn apart and will suffer greatly. Know the river has its destination. The elders say we must let go of the shore, push off into the middle of the river, keep our eyes open, and our heads above water. And I say, see who is in there with you, and celebrate.

At this time in history, we are to take nothing personally. Least of all, ourselves. For the moment that we do, our spiritual growth and journey comes to a halt.

The time of the lone wolf is over. Gather yourselves! Banish the word struggle from your attitude and your vocabulary. All that we do now must be done in a sacred manner and in celebration. We are the Ones we've been waiting for.

Push off into the middle of the river, into your dreams. Look who is in the river with you. Don't feel you have to do it alone. Gather together in a sacred manner. Honor and celebrate your dreams. The unfolding of your heart dreams, your holy dreams, is what you've been waiting for.

In 1986, I (Margaret) journeyed to the Soviet Union with Citizen Diplomats for Peace, an organization founded by Rama Vernon, a well-known visionary who dreams of peace for the world. She creates opportunities for people of different countries, cultures, and beliefs to meet and get to know one another, to cease fearing one another, and to build trust. Our group consisted of healers, including clergy, medical doctors, scientists, and therapists, and the goal was to meet with our counterparts in Russia. The tour group host was Alan Cohen, author of *I Had It All The Time.*[2]

The journey began in Finland where our group spent time blending together, getting to know one another, and envisioning our mission, which was to bring love, good will, and open hearts to Russia. We prayed and meditated together and were blessed every day by the musical feasts of singer/songwriter, Charley Thweatt. Finland was bright, sunny, and clean, with lavish food and lovely hotel rooms. After three days in this wonderful country with lots of great energy from the group, we were full of excitement and laughter as we boarded the night train to Moscow, ready for a new adventure. We easily fell asleep to the gentle rocking motion of the train.

As dawn broke, some of us rose, still in pajamas, and gathered outside of our compartments in the hallway to look out the windows as the train pulled into the Moscow station. The sky was overcast and dreary. People stood on the perimeter of the depot in drizzling rain, huddled around fires warming themselves. The scene was familiar, like street people in Washington, D.C., our nation's capitol. We dressed quietly, lost in our own thoughts, and prepared our luggage for inspection by the border guards. The mood of the group had shifted drastically. Many of us became somber and quiet. The great feeling we had shared the night before changed.

Some of us began to feel an anxious, foreboding feeling.

As we looked at the uniformed guards, we noticed that their arms were crossed and they appeared to be "scowling" at us. I'm sure that we appeared to be less than friendly to them as well. Some of our group reverted back to an old view of seeing Russians as the "enemy." We were all of the age to remember fears concerning the "cold war" and old anxieties resurfaced.

For me, my memories took me back to age twelve, sixth grade, and the "duck and cover" A-bomb drills. I remembered the "Red Scare" and accompanying my parents on Sundays after church to look at bomb shelters, which were for sale in shopping center parking lots!

What had been an experience of "love and light" and fearlessness one day in Finland was now transformed into fearful thoughts, a consciousness of "us and them"; us and "the enemy." The real enemy, of course, was our fear.

The luggage inspectors finished their jobs and most of us passed without having anything confiscated. We debarked from the train and dragged tons of luggage behind. Like many American tourists, most of us had way too much! Literally and energetically, we were heavily burdened. We cautiously peered at the guards, as they appeared to be watching our every move. No one spoke; neither us nor them, and no one dared smile.

Then, one among us dared to dream a holier outcome! Michael, a fellow in our group, age twenty-one, whose experience in this lifetime included Down's syndrome, saved the day! This sweet, innocent, young man came through for us in this seemingly "dark" moment. As we marched along somberly, heads held down, Michael burst out singing "God

Bless America"! Of course, we were all stunned. Then, we began to laugh, including the Soviet guards! Faces lit up, spirits lifted, bodies relaxed, luggage no longer felt as heavy, and most importantly, our emotional baggage lightened. God Bless Michael—our Hero!

It took one among us to remember, that's all. Just one to raise the energy of the whole group. We knew only a few words of Russian but were able to communicate with our eyes, smiles, and handshakes. The guards spoke mostly one word to us, over and over, "Mir . . . Mir," as they shook our hands and looked into our eyes. "Peace, Peace." I'll never forget what "Mir" means now. The rest of our tour was filled with serendipity, heart-to-heart meetings, and embracing each other. Not "us and them," but people attempting to heal old fears and understand each other.

Marcel Vogel, an IBM scientist in the early days of computer research (and for those of us from the sixties, he also invented day-glow paint), used to teach about the following phenomenon: When a high resonating crystal is placed in a room and lower resonating crystals are placed around it, the lower resonating crystals will raise their frequency to match that of the higher resonating crystal. It takes one person to hold the higher vision, the higher perspective, as Michael did, and the rest of us will begin to move into that higher vision. Isn't it magnificent how that works!

Dreaming the holiest dreams for ourselves, for others, for our country, and the planet is one of the most important things we can do in our lives. Holding Holy Vision every day for the dream you wish to create is of vital importance. This means to be as clear as you can be that your dream is the highest and best for your life. It's very important to be sure that the vision you're holding for yourself or anyone else is a holy vision. One that holds an intention for good for all involved. Then, trust that God is participating in your dream, pray for it unceasingly, see yourself lovingly supported in the creation of your dream and ultimately living that dream in joy, peace, and harmony.

Always remember what the Christ said to us a long time ago: "You can do all of the things I have done and greater. . . ." This means we have unlimited capabilities when we live in trust and believe in greater possibilities for ourselves.

Margaret and I have witnessed so many miracles in our lives and in our work that we absolutely believe all things are possible. Holding this belief in our hearts is a grand and wondrous blessing. Miracles are created from the holy visions we hold dearly in our hearts.

Sometimes, the visions that we hold come from a place of fear. Then, we forget about the greater possibilities. We forget that the Divine is always with us, holding the holiest vision for us when we are in doubt. When we are afraid and forget about holy vision, our doubts begin to magnify, and soon the field of creative possibilities gets smaller and smaller as the fear grows. This leaves us feeling weak and more focused on the impossible. This is a time when it is imperative to ask for help so that we can shift to a more holy place—our hearts—where greater possibilities live. This support comes from both the Divine that lives within us, as well as other people who we feel can be loving and helpful to us when we are in doubt or fear. This can be a literal calling forth of a support team, a vision team to help us feel and see more clearly the holy healing visions of the heart.

How many of you know yourselves to be visionaries?

Well, for anyone that may doubt how powerful you are as a visionary, then I, David, have a story for you. The story illustrates how incredibly powerful you truly are and what is possible for you to create.

A few years ago Margaret and I did a weekend retreat in Idyllwild, California. The theme of the retreat was "Creating Our Heart Visions." Twenty-five people gathered together to talk about their hearts' desires, to support and encourage each other to believe in greater possibilities, and to literally take the steps necessary to manifest dreams.

Kim, one of the women in the retreat, was really having a difficult time staying present with the others and seemed distant and depressed. We asked her what was going on and she said, "I'm afraid because my friend has been diagnosed with a rare kind of terminal cancer. It started as an open sore on her lip and the doctors say this type of cancer cannot be stopped. It invades the entire body, the blood, and the skin cells. My fear is that she will not make it through this. I'm really having a hard time getting involved in the retreat because all I can think about is her." It was obvious that Kim was distraught, and her fearful thoughts were keeping her from receiving the comfort and encouragement of the group.

We asked if she would accept our support in holding another kind of vision for her friend. She said yes, so we asked her to shift her focus to her breath, to breathe gently and easily, and to call on Divine Spirit to ease her thoughts and tension and move healing energy into her heart. As she concentrated on her breathing, she became more present and relaxed. We asked her to imagine the holiest dream possible for her friend, what we call a "high holy vision" or a "remarkable outcome."

Kim took some more deep breaths, thought about this for a few moments, and then very calmly described her highest and holiest vision for her friend. She said, "The vision in my heart is that when she goes to the hospital for another biopsy, she will be healed, completely 100% cancer-free, and will walk out of the hospital feeling happy and fully blessed."

Wow, what a powerful vision! What a shift in thinking! We asked her, "In your heart of hearts, do you really believe this is possible?" She thought for a moment and answered, "Yes, in my heart of hearts I believe this is possible!" We asked the rest of the group the same question. One by one each participant answered, "Yes, I believe this is possible." We all gathered in a circle, held hands, prayed, and held this holy vision with Kim for her friend's healing. In that moment, we were a team of loving supportive visionaries who saw the possibilities for health and perfection.

After the prayer we all felt a deep sense of peace. Kim was then able to be fully present, her heart wide open, and she was at peace for the rest of the retreat.

We all went home on Monday, and that night Margaret and I got a call from Kim. She told us this amazing story:

Her friend had gone to the hospital on Monday, the day after our retreat, for another biopsy. Much to the doctor's amazement, the cancer was gone! The skin on her lip was completely smooth, as if there had never been any cancer. Upon hearing the news, her heart was filled with gratitude and she knew she had been blessed. Later that day she left the hospital 100% cancer-free, fulfilling the holy vision.

That is how powerful all of you are! That's what we all are capable of creating, sometimes in the blink of an eye! When we hold holy vision in our hearts, possibilities for remarkable outcomes expand and miracles can happen.

Margaret and I would like you to know that we are on your vision team, holding the holy vision with you for many blessings of love, healing, abundance, and support. So dream the holiest dream and believe in miracles because *You* are God's holiest dream and that is the greatest miracle of all!

Exercise to
Dream a Holy Dream

First and foremost, it is essential to envision your dream from the heart where holy dreams are birthed. This enables you to be focused and clear about your vision and opens the channels for greater possibilities to be created. The following is a sacred process to envision your holy dream:

✧ Create a peaceful, sacred environment, free from distractions. Light a candle, play some soft relaxing music, and sit quietly in a comfortable position. You could also choose to lie down if you wish.

✧ Take a few deep breaths. Imagine breathing holy God-breaths into your heart. This helps to free the mind of distracting thoughts. If you do have these thoughts, just bless them and continue focusing on the God-breath.

✧ As you become more calm and centered, call on your Heavenly support team to be with you in this process— angels, holy ones, whoever helps you to feel supported, peaceful, and comforted. If you are not aware of a Heavenly support team, then imagine what it would be like to have one. See these beloveds surrounding you and acting as holy witnesses to your dream.

✧ Feel the support and love of these witnesses. Relax and continue to breathe.

✧ Imagine you are standing in a sacred sanctuary within your heart. Beautiful plants, trees, and multicolored flowers surround you. Everywhere you look there are magnificent angels smiling at you and welcoming you in this holy space.

✧ Feel the exquisite peace of this moment.

✧ Now, notice a beautiful, purple light in the form of an infinity symbol (∞) radiating on the ground in the middle of your sanctuary. You are fascinated by this exquisite light and are drawn to the infinity symbol. As you walk toward it, a beautiful angel appears within one side of the symbol and looks at you with warm and welcoming eyes. The angel tells you that this is your dream symbol and he or she has come to support you in envisioning your holy dream. Your angel then invites you to step into the other side of the infinity symbol and reaches out to take your hand to support you in taking this most important step.

✧ With great anticipation, you take the angel's hand and step inside. You are immediately filled with an exquisite healing light. Every cell of your being is nourished in a sweet elixir of divine energy. You feel so loved, so peaceful, that you relax, let go of all thoughts, and allow yourself to be blessed.

✧ Your angel tells you that your sacred infinity symbol is designed to help you feel inspired so that you can easily envision your holy dream.

✧ Take this knowing into your heart and allow yourself to feel a great inspiration stirring within you.

✧ Now, from your heart, call forth the vision of your holy dream. Picture your heart's desire, something that lifts your spirit, makes your heart sing, something you feel is the highest and best for you, and from which you and others can benefit.

✧ Some of you will get a picture of this vision; some will get a feeling or knowing about it. Whatever your method of receiving is, simply allow it to unfold. As your picture or knowing manifests, view it with an open heart, and if necessary, ask for clarity until you feel satisfied it is the clearest vision for you, one that lifts your spirit.

✧ See and/or feel yourself happily involved in your dream, smiling, joyous, in complete harmony with all aspects of the dream. Know that your angel is acting as a holy witness, a great visionary that is holding the dream with you.

✧ See yourself being supported by friends and colleagues in the creation of your dream. Picture yourself stepping into the dream and becoming an integral part of it. Breathe life into your dream. What are the colors of your dream? What do you feel about your dream?

✧ Spend a few minutes immersed in your dream. Imagine yourself living that dream—happy, content, and knowing that you absolutely deserve this blessing.

✧ When you are ready, give great thanks to your angel, knowing that he or she is always with you.

✧ Honor your dream infinity symbol and gently bring yourself back into the present moment feeling refreshed, excited, and full of inspiration.

Every day remind yourself of your holy dream in your thoughts, prayers, and meditations. Call those friends, family, and colleagues who would be truly supportive of your dream, and ask them to envision it with you. Remember that your angel is on your team!

Many Blessings to you and all of your dreams.

AS WE PERCEIVE, SO SHALL WE RECEIVE

There is more to 20/20 vision than meets the eye! Seeing our life through the eyes of the Divine is of vital importance. As we perceive, so shall we receive. Consider what you are dreaming about. What do you envision for that dream? Are you looking at it with great enthusiasm (meaning "with God"), or do you see it with quiet resignation? Is your dream believable or do you have doubts about it? Do you have faith that your dream is achievable or does it seem impossible to you? Well, what you see is what you get!

Your thoughts are exceptionally powerful and can create amazing results. Positive thoughts create productive results, and negative thoughts create doubt and despair. We tremendously increase the possibilities of creating our dreams by continuously holding the highest and holiest vision in our heart. Heart visions are not limited! We can reach for the sky because all things are possible in our hearts. Simply believing that something you desire is possible can literally manifest it because your heart is open to that possibility.

I have worn glasses since I was six years old in the first grade. Most of us who have worn glasses remember the kidding we got from some of the children at school and how that made us feel. One of the things I heard a lot was, "David, you sure look funny with four eyes!" Some of us learned how to hide behind our glasses because we were not being seen for who we truly were, and it felt like we needed to protect ourselves from the world. We then began to see ourselves through other peoples' eyes.

To a certain extent, that was the case for me, and I became very shy and introverted in the classroom. Interestingly, however, I turned to sports to be more recognized. I was very athletic and never wore my glasses while playing sports. I felt so much better about myself then and received a lot of acceptance and encouragement. This, of course, allowed me to see myself in a whole new light!

This "inner sight" also helped me excel at sports even though I had difficulty actually seeing—either the ball or the other players—without my glasses! I developed a kind of inner instinct to move or react at just the right time to succeed at what I was doing. By the time I graduated from college that inner instinct was highly developed. It helped me to be much more extroverted even though I was still wearing glasses and sometimes hiding behind them when I felt uncomfortable in another's presence.

I dreamed that one day a miracle would happen and I would no longer need to wear glasses, that I would have 20/20 vision—perfect eyesight. I knew that this was possible if I continued to develop my inner vision, improve my view of myself, and trust that others could see me more truthfully (as I revealed myself to them more truthfully) whether I wore glasses or not. I began to dream a holier dream, seeing with 20/20 vision both from the inner as well as the outer! I believed that this was possible.

Well, guess what! In October of 2001, about six weeks after the 9/11 tragedy, we were presenting a Sunday service at a church in Ventura, California. I had just finished talking about a powerful healing and forgiveness process I had experienced at a workshop on letting go of old wounds, when a man walked up to me, shook my hand, and told me he felt really inspired by what I said. I held his hand for a minute, looked into his eyes, and felt genuinely acknowledged. I was delighted that my words had touched him.

He then said, "My name is Dr. Paul Dougherty. I'm a laser eye surgeon and medical director of Dougherty Laser Vision in Camarillo, California, and I feel truly inspired to give you a gift! I noticed that you were wearing glasses during your talk and figured you have probably worn them for a long time. Is that true?"

"Yes," I answered, "since I was six years old."

Then I noticed the twinkle in his eyes as he said, "I would like to give you the gift of laser eye surgery so you can have 20/20 vision."

Well, I was stunned and couldn't speak for a couple of seconds! All kinds of thoughts swirled around in my head. Finally, I regained my composure enough to answer a resounding, "Yes, thank you so much, you're an answer to my prayer! I've been dreaming about this for a long time." God sent me an Earth angel to answer my prayers! Paul asked me to come to his office in a couple of days to determine if I was a good candidate for this procedure and I agreed. I could hardly wait to "see" if this was going to work for me, and when the time came, I felt a tremendous excitement.

I arrived at his office and was greeted by very warm and

friendly people who made me feel right at home. Everyone was very attentive, which gave me a real sense of security. After all, these were my eyes that were going to be operated on, and I was feeling a little nervous, so the tender loving care was most appreciated! Several of the doctor's assistants checked my eyes, and then Paul came in, looked at my eyes, said that I was a perfect candidate for laser surgery, and that I would be seeing 20/20 very soon. Those words were music to my ears! I was so excited I could hardly contain myself! Paul was so confident, I felt absolutely reassured that I was in good hands, and all my nervousness just melted away.

The next day I returned to the clinic to have the laser procedure done. Margaret came with me for support, but little did she know that she would actually be able to witness the surgery. What a gift! After I was prepped for surgery, Paul told me again that everything was going to be fine, that he would talk me through the entire surgery, and tell me how it was going every step of the way. Again, I felt very reassured and comforted and I said, "I'm ready, let's do it."

The laser surgery was amazing to me. I didn't feel any pain, and Paul talked to me the whole time, which was probably about five minutes for each eye. He kept saying really positive things like, "It's going perfectly. You're doing great, Dave. You'll be seeing 20/20 real soon." I never knew surgery could actually be a pleasant experience!

First, the doctor numbed my eyes with eye drops. Then he used a Keratone, an instrument devised to separate the front layer of the cornea from the rest of the eye to create the corneal flap. The flap was then folded over and an Excimer laser was used to reshape the tissue underneath it.

This procedure is quite like sculpting a contact lens on the eye. Then the flap was put back into place where it began to heal immediately and naturally without stitches.

Margaret, who was in the next room, was grateful for the opportunity to watch this entire amazing procedure through a large glass window. What a gift to be able to see this miracle of science performed right before her eyes! After the surgery was over, Paul examined my eyes again and said everything looked great. He told me to go back to our motel and lie down, keeping my eyes closed and covered with protective goggles for the next four hours. Then I could open them to a whole new world!

It seemed like those four hours took an eternity but finally the moment of truth arrived! I slowly took the goggles off, said a prayer and opened my eyes. Lo and behold, I could see perfectly for the first time in my life! I was astonished. It was one of the most precious moments of my life. I'll never forget seeing things so clearly—shapes, colors, words—everything was clearer. I started jumping up and down on the bed like a kid in a candy store, looking at myself in the mirror and seeing one happy camper! I started singing some crazy song that I made up on the spot—I do that sometimes—and that always makes Margaret laugh. We held each other in absolute delight. Later that day we went out to get some sunglasses for me. I'd never worn non-prescription sunglasses before that I could actually see through, and this was a real treat. I started reading various road signs and saw words that even Margaret couldn't see, and she has great long-distance vision. We both got a big kick out of that.

A few days later I spent some time reflecting on what a

phenomenal gift it was to receive clear outer vision. I believe the gift came to me because I really worked on self-forgiveness for seeing myself through others' eyes, for letting that affect me so much and sometimes closing down. Forgiveness opened my heart to seeing myself through the eyes of love, thus allowing others the freedom to look more deeply into my eyes, right into my heart and soul. After all, The eyes are the mirrors of the soul, the spiritual, holy, eternal aspect of our being!

I want to thank everyone at Dougherty Laser Vision for their kindness and professionalism and a very special "thank you" to Dr. Paul for the exquisite gift he gave me, for being such a great doctor, and even more importantly, for his heart of gold.

How are you "seeing" your life? Are you looking from the inside out, or are you seeing yourself from the outside in, through others' eyes? Are you seeing your dreams through 20/20 vision or do they appear distorted and clouded by feelings of self-doubt? Are you hiding in this doubt? God always sees the Divinity of who we are—the Divine self. God does not judge us, but instead urges us to shine and to view our lives through the clearest and holiest vision. When we make the shift into a loving heart-perception of self and see the good in the world, miracles happen! Earth angels show up for us and give us blessings. Remember, as we perceive, so shall we receive!

One of the greatest parts of this story that I (Margaret) got to witness so beautifully was that David *really believed* his dream was possible. For several years he would periodically say, "One day I'm going to have laser surgery and see with 20/20 vision." He saw in his mind's eye and knew in his heart that 20/20 vision was truly a possibility, and he "held the vision" for a long time.

One of the most important considerations in creating our dreams is our "possibility list," the essence of which is formed by our beliefs and positive thoughts, coupled with our creative ideas, hopes, and the steps we are taking toward manifesting that dream. The possibility list is a picture of our faith in the dream. *Faith* is the "substance," the energetic building material, the "evidence," or "proof" that the dream is on its way toward manifestation. Faith affects what and how we see and how pieces or fragments of the dream are attracted to us, such as, connections with people, opportunities, information, so-called coincidences, and intuitive ideas.

There is another kind of list that most of us have had some experience with: the "what if" list. There are both positive and not so positive "what if's." The positive elements are the action steps for clarity and planning of our dream. Things like, "What if I need more education or research for this dream to unfold?" or, "What if more money is needed for advertising?" or, "What if my tux no longer fits when it's time to accept the award for my invention?" These kinds of questions are valuable as they guide us to move forward. They are not stumbling blocks, but rather our creative mind working with the unfolding dream and putting the elements in place to "cover all the bases."

I recently read this quote on a greeting card from Tomato Cards, DCI Studios: "To accomplish great things, we must not only act but Dream, not only plan, but Believe."

The other kind of "what if" list keeps bombarding us with thoughts of what can go wrong. Rather than seeing creative possibilities, we can get "blind-sided" by doubt.

That can lead us to give up the dream altogether, or shut down the creative energy that is attempting to flow into our consciousness.

Edgar Mitchell, former astronaut and founder of Noetic Sciences Institute, tells a story about the debate years ago over the idea of putting a man on the moon. One group of learned scientists said, "It's impossible, a waste of time, energy, and money to even consider it."

Then another group of equally brilliant scientists asked the most important and essential question: "*What if it is possible? And, if it is, how will we do it?*"

The obvious difference between these two groups of scientists was the "what if." One group was stuck in non-belief and non-movement; the other was opened to forward movement. This way opened the door to the great reservoir of creative possibilities.

Do you believe your dream is possible, and if so, how will you create it? Or, are you and your dream being unhinged by negative "what if" lists? If the latter is so, you need to move the energy! Ways to move energy include prayer, research, and taking one action step at a time, for instance, getting brochures for that trip to Bali, or picking up the college catalog, or writing your business plan, or asking for support.

Several years ago I (Margaret) had a dream to widen the scope of my teaching work, not only to lecture in churches and conferences, but hospitals, mental health agencies, and colleges as well. I had a "what if" list about three miles long. What if my credentials weren't good enough? What if they think I don't know what I'm talking about? What if I really *don't* know what I'm talking about! What if, what if, what if? I began to realize that I'd lived with a "what if" list much of my life. Even though I felt good about myself in many ways, I still had this nagging message that resounded in my head whenever I began to do something I'd never done before. The message was, "You don't know how to do this. What if you try and fail?" And that question would keep me stuck, paralyzed in doubt. I'm not talking about that glorious place of stillness where you rest and listen and wait for the next right step. I'm talking about stagnation!

Then, Eureka! I remembered that David, my beloved, is a great coach in helping people break through old patterns of resistance. So, I confessed to him that I was still living my life with a "what if" list fueled by fear rather than creativity. I explained that I wanted to live with trust, trust in myself and trust for God's guidance in my life.

David went into deep meditation (for about a millisecond!) and then enthusiastically announced, "I know! We'll go shoot rapids in a canoe on the Colorado River!" I said, "No way, José. There's gotta be another way!" (To clarify, the word is *rapids*. A woman who heard me tell this story in her church approached me after the service and said, "*YOU* shot rabbits? From a canoe?!!")

So, there we were on the Colorado River, thirty eager people in fifteen canoes, happily floating down the river, paddling and splashing each other with water. As we approached the first rapid, our guide, Bob, shouted, "Eddy in!" (Meaning, "Pull over to the bank of the river.")

We beached our canoes, walked around the bend and looked at the first rapid. (I'm a Sagittarian so I always appreciate seeing where I'm going before I get there.) Aghast, I looked at the whirling waters of a huge rapid, a fallen tree swirling around right in the middle of it, and said, "You've got to be kidding!" I whipped out my brochure and emphatically reminded our guide that this was *supposed* to be a Class 1, Beginner Level canoe trip.

He said, "Yeah, and this is the only rapid on this stretch of the river that's not a Class 1."

I asked, "Well, what is it?"

"A Class 3" he answered.

"But this is the *first* one," I moaned, as I walked away in disbelief.

Have you ever noticed how the Universe makes things more interesting when we're breaking through fears? Well, much to my chagrin, it was also raining and lightning! I diplomatically suggested to our fearless leader that we turn around and go back to where we put our canoes in the river that morning and start again when the storm was over. Bob, who is also a Course in Miracles teacher, gave me the perfect metaphysical response: "We never go back on the river." "Right!" I blipped at him and marched off to find David who would surely agree that this new adventure was far too scary and that we'd better turn around.

To make the whole experience even *more* interesting, the name of the rapid was "The Hail Mary!" Although I wasn't raised Catholic, I've always had a great appreciation for the ceremony and ritual and the way Catholics hold a space for the miraculous, especially through stories of the Saints. When I went to Medjugore in Yugoslavia in 1989, I became "Catholic for a week" and learned the "Hail Mary." Now would be a good time, I thought, to say that prayer!

I looked at David and said, "We're not going through that rapid are we? It's raining. It's lightning. And it's called the Hail Mary, for God's Sake!" Trying to subtly influence his answer, I kept swinging my head back and forth in a "No" as I waited for his response.

David threw his hands up in the air and with great enthusiasm proclaimed, "This is the whole reason we came!"

"Right!" I said, and marched off to find my dear sister, Pam.

I was still vigorously shaking my head when I approached her, hoping that she would get the message, "We're not going through that rapid, are we?"

My sister started jumping up and down, laughing, and said, "Margaret, this is the most fun part!"

She thought the idea of shooting this giant rapid was terrific. I thought it was terrifying! "Terrific" and "terrifying"—same root word, huge life energy, and very different perspectives.

I'm five years older than Pam, and we were raised in the same house with the same parents, both of whom we love dearly. My precious Southern mother is one of my greatest voices of support and "Go For It" energy. But when I was growing up I learned from her to be very cautious about anything I did with my physical body. I was quite often told, "Be careful or you'll get hurt." It was a different story with Pam, who is rather fearless. She goes downhill skiing and scuba diving as though she received a totally different message. Sort of like being raised by two different mothers!

At this particular moment, I was thoroughly stuck in an "early life" pattern, and as I perceived the situation, I determined that my physical body was in mortal danger! Then I glanced over my shoulder and watched two fellows, who had been on this same stretch of the river the year before, as they carried their canoe around the bend, making their way along the bank and completely bypassing the rapid. That was it, an undeniable clue!

Finally, I approached my canoe partner for the day, a great guy named Hal, and whined, "Hal, we're not going through this rapid, are we? It's raining and lightning. It's called the Hail Mary." I grimaced and even stomped my foot. I waited for him to agree and "get out of Dodge" with me. Instead, he became the voice of courage that helped me break through the fear.

He said, "Margaret, this time last year I was diagnosed with a life-threatening brain tumor. I called you and David and asked you to pray with me. You agreed and you also advised me to call together a team of twelve people to hold the highest and holiest vision of healing for me. You and David were on that team. We all made an agreement that my healing experience would be the most amazing, miraculous time of my entire life journey, and that is the way it unfolded. That experience brought more good, more miracles, more love, more awakening to me than any other experience of my entire life."

Well, what could I say to that? My "inner attorney" had just lost the case. I knew that shooting a rapid in a canoe was going to be a whole lot easier than what Hal had lived through, and I knew it was "now or never" for me. I had to break through that stuck place of fear then and there! So, I "suited up" in my life jacket, grabbed my paddle, and jumped into the front of the canoe. Hal and I eddied back out into the middle of the river and caught the current. I squealed all the way as we paddled for dear life, maneuvering our canoe through the wild and mighty "Hail Mary!" And we did it! We survived!

Certainly, I know that life gets a whole lot harder and way more frightening than shooting a rapid in a canoe. Of course it does! Many of us have maneuvered through some really scary life challenges. My "Hail Mary" experience, however, made me aware of *how* I had often approached difficult times. My old pattern was this: If something looked like it was going to be too hard or scary for me, I would "check out" and not be totally present, I'd "paddle my canoe" but wouldn't be fully attentive to what the Divine was offering me in those challenges. I would shut down and miss the opportunity of seeing or hearing or feeling the fullness of the experience, sometimes not even remembering or seeing God's Presence in the midst of it.

After the adrenaline rush of the "Hail Mary" wore off, I began reflecting on these insights. My mind quieted and I became still. Easy to do because we were now on a stretch of the river that was calm. Our normally boisterous group was quietly and effortlessly paddling, allowing the gentle current to move the canoes along. I no longer felt fear. My body and mind were at ease.

Suddenly, as I raised the paddle to take another stroke, a Ruby-throated hummingbird landed on my left arm. I'll never forget that moment. It seemed like the most natural occurrence in the world. The little hummer, who can move more rapidly than the rushing water I'd just wrestled, brought the gift of stillness. He spread his little wings and sat quietly. Time "stood still" as many in the group witnessed this amazing visit. Maybe he was resting or drying off his little wings. Maybe his mission was to bring us the gift of stillness and the awareness that we truly are part of the ever-continuing stream of life, living the one eternal moment.

After about a minute, the little hummer lifted up, flew over to David who was in a different canoe, hovered in front of his face for a few seconds, and then shot off into the desert. Was that coincidence, or was he following a line of energy that connects David and me? I believe the latter. We like to think that somewhere in the Colorado desert there is a hummingbird holding the vision for us, whether we're shooting Hail Mary's or paddling gently down the stream— Merrily, merrily, merrily, merrily, Life is but a Dream.

The hummingbird also reminded me that there are always gifts available to us when we are willing to be present and available to Spirit during every life experience. Even, perhaps, most especially during the difficult and challenging ones. The way we perceive our "Hail Mary's" makes all the difference—terrifying or terrific, nightmare or holy dream.

God is always present with us. How magnificent and complete it is when we decide to also be present with God. Then we can "see" perfectly and without fear all the good that visits our lives.

Moving Through "Hail Mary's" with 20/20 Vision

✧ Sit quietly in a comfortable chair in a peaceful environment. Close your eyes, if you wish, and take three deep
God-breaths to calm and center yourself. Continue to
breathe gently and think of a time in the recent past
when you were confronted with a challenge, a "Hail
Mary." Take another deep breath and picture yourself in
this experience as if you are watching a movie.

✧ Take note of everything and everyone involved in your
movie. Then notice how you are feeling in this situation.
Allow yourself to feel these feelings and continue to
breathe. What are you thinking about as you review each
frame of the film? Take a couple of minutes to "see" how
your thoughts are affecting your feelings.

✧ Now shift your focus back to your breath. Breathe ever so
gently and relax. Call on the Holy Spirit to bathe your
heart in a beautiful lavender healing light. Picture this
light filling your heart with the purest, sweetest love you
can imagine. See yourself becoming more and more
relaxed as you allow the purity of Spirit to soothe and
calm you. Picture or imagine any fear or trepidation you
might have felt as simply being melted away by the lavender light. Feel yourself getting stronger and stronger.

✧ Call forth an angel to be with you now. It can be a
heavenly angel or someone you know to be an Earthly

angel. Take the hand of your angel and imagine yourself moving through that "Hail Mary" with lots of courage and "Go For It" energy. Clearly see the empowered, Divine You moving forward without fear.

✧ Feel the power of who you truly are in every cell of your being. Now imagine that you have gone through the "Hail Mary," you're on the other side of it, and you feel great! And then a hummingbird lands on your arm and brings you the wonderful gift of eternal stillness. Spend a few minutes in this exquisite stillness. Then take another deep God-breath and slowly begin to open your eyes.

✧ Perceiving yourself through "20/20" vision always brings you a great gift, so get ready to receive it!

PLEASE DON'T QUIT!
YOUR PRESENCE IS
IMPORTANT

"Margaret! Keep peddling!" My older sister, Joan, was teaching me to ride and for the hundredth time she pushed me on her rickety, blue bike down the black tar road—and then let go! Neighborhood kids who had already been through this rite of passage moved out of the way, yelling, "Here she comes!"

Learning to ride a bike was thrilling and frightening! Momentum was the key, stopping gracefully the goal, and scabbed knees were a given. If children played in the street, roller-skating or riding a bike, they had cuts and bruises. It was expected. I'd stop and go, stop and go, weave and fall. Then again, I'd stand and straddle the bike and Joan would hold it steady as I placed my feet on the pedals. Then she would run alongside and push as I pedaled, pushing and running, pushing and running, until she'd let go and yell, "Keep pedaling! Don't stop!"

Life can be just like riding that bike. Sometimes we lose our momentum, get confused or tired, have too many "scabs," and we stop peddling. It's important to follow the natural rhythms of our bodies and emotions. Honoring the need for rest and renewal is essential for a balanced life.

A few years ago, when I was weary from a heavy travel schedule, stopping for rest almost turned into quitting altogether. Did you ever feel like quitting, meaning, to cease believing that your presence and actions make a difference in the world?

One afternoon I was resting and did one of my favorite spiritual practices—tuning into the Oprah Winfrey Show! But on this particular day, instead of Oprah, there was a frightening news report about a very angry stockbroker who walked into an Atlanta office building and opened fire on his colleagues. I immediately called my niece who worked in downtown Atlanta. Unable to reach her, I began to pray. Distraught and worried, I sat on the bed for a long time, weeping tears of anguish for the human family.

I wailed, "What is happening to our world?" Then I turned to David and said, "You know, I've been in ministry and healing work, and have been a counselor and teacher for all these years, praying and holding the vision for healing, but it's not working! It's not making a difference—so I quit! I quit!"

My beloved partner, David, did the most precious thing. He opened our calendar and said, "Okay, how much time do we need to block out for rest and renewal? A day, a week?" Emphatically, I said, "You don't get it. I quit! It's just not working!" Well, God definitely has a sense of humor because at that moment the phone rang. Now if you don't think Spirit is listening, just hear this:

I picked up the phone and said in a gruff, angry voice "HELLO!" You see, I had quit! Otherwise, I would have said "Hel-lo" in a lovely lilting voice. But I had quit. And the woman said, "You won't remember me. Two years ago in Hemet, California, you and David did a workshop at our church. My husband and I were close to divorce and our teenagers were in a lot of trouble. Our finances were really pitiful and you both agreed to be on our vision team.

After the counseling session, you joined us in prayer and held the holy vision that there would be healing and renewal in each one of those areas. Well let me tell you, my marriage is healing beautifully. My teenagers are continually doing better. We feel like a close family again and our finances are being restored to a healthy place. I've been meaning to call you for two years now to thank you for your work and also to say, 'Please don't ever quit!'"

"Don't Quit!" Now, if she had called me six months before and said these things, it would have been nice. If she had said to me, "What a great workshop. Hope you come back again sometime," that would have been sweet. Thankfully, we hear those kinds of messages. But instead she said the very words, the enlivening words, my soul needed to hear the most! "Don't quit!" Spirit is listening, folks!

I have talked with a number of people who are thinking of quitting in many different ways. Maybe you have had that thought, or someone close to you has stopped believing that his or her presence in the world is important. I know there can be weariness and questions like, "What good is prayer or visioning or taking action for world peace doing?" I know there are thoughts of quitting because I've been there myself—more than once.

So my message to you, and more importantly, Spirit's message to you is, "Please don't quit." Now more than ever, the world needs visionaries, people of prayer and wise action, people dreaming the Holiest Dreams rather than dreams of fear.

We can convert any kind of life experience, even the most painful moments that someone intended for harm, like September 11th, into a catalyst for healing, awakening, and creating outcomes of ultimate good for humankind. The question is, Can we hold fast and see the spectacular Presence and possibility for good in every moment? Can we see both dark and painful moments and bright and easy moments all as opportunities for the human family to evolve?

In his book *How, Then, Shall We Live?* Wayne Muller writes, "All through the day there are these singular moments when it is time for change, time for something to be set free."[3] These moments of change, these opportunities for shifts in our thinking and the way we live, are seen more often and more clearly if, rather than quit, we do as the Buddhists suggest: "Wake Up, Stay Present, and Pay Attention." Thankfully, I was awake and paying attention for a recent "singular moment."

On September 9, 2001, after presenting a Sunday service and an afternoon workshop at a church in Oregon, my voice got raspier and raspier and by that night, I was speaking to David in whispers. I had never lost my voice before in all my twenty years of public speaking! Then, of course, on September 11th, a worldwide scream shook us all.

A few days later, I made an appointment for a healing session with a Rabbi friend in Ashland, Oregon, where we live. I know him to be a faith-keeper who works closely with the presence of Christ. He has the ability to keep seeing Spirit at work even in the midst of chaos, and holds that Holy Vision for others when they have forgotten. I asked him to do a healing ceremony with me, partly to restore my voice, and also because I needed the extra support in seeing good at work in the midst of painful world events.

Upon entering his home I quietly removed my shoes and was greeted by a little girl, age two, who was visiting my friend. We looked at each other for a few seconds, and then she stretched out on the floor, belly down, placed her hands on my feet and rested her head on her hands. She stayed there, face down, for several minutes. Bewildered, I choked out a whisper to her mother; "She must be mesmerized by my brightly-colored toenails." Her mother said, "She's been around lots of brightly-colored toenails. This is definitely something else."

I tell you, I stood still for about five minutes witnessing this remarkable event. I wanted to say something, but of course speaking was difficult! So, I just relaxed and received her touch as a healing blessing. One of my great teachers, Hilda Charlton, used to say that the New Millennium is one of the most incredible times to be alive on the planet and that the angels delight in us and kneel at our feet, blessing us for making the decision to be alive at such a time!

Finally, this "angel" child stood up, smiled at me, and happily began playing by herself. It seemed to me that I had already received a healing ceremony, but kept my appointment with the Rabbi anyway. I experienced another powerful healing session and gratefully paid him. Later I thought, *Maybe I should have paid the little girl as well!*

It is good to remember, especially in times of chaos or challenge, that we are not alone. There are blessings and healings, "angels and faith-keepers," always available to us from both the seen and the unseen, most particularly when we are weary and want to quit; or when we are called to reassess our thinking and make remarkable choices, choices that could help transform painful patterns of fear and survival in our personal lives, and which can then affect others with whom we are connected.

During my days without a voice, Spirit invited me into silence. Of course, like so many people, I began praying unceasingly after 9/11, and the inability to speak became a kind of gift to me. Since my work involves a lot of public speaking, I received a great blessing in the sanctuary of silence, reflecting on some hard questions:

✧ Are my words creating love, concern, and compassion, or fear, anger, and prejudice?

✧ Are my thoughts and actions terrorizing to me or others?

✧ Are my voice and presence working for or against the good evolving in the world?

Esther, whose story is told in the Old Testament, used her voice and presence for the good during another time of terrorism. She was a Jewish woman who became a Queen. This was remarkable since her husband, the King, was not Jewish and had a history of persecuting the Jews.

One day, Esther's Uncle Mordecai came to visit and gave her a message of encouragement and insight. She had an amazing opportunity to speak out on behalf of the Jews who were being killed by the King's general. Mordecai said to Esther, "Who knows whether thou art come to the kingdom for such a time as this?" He was her faith-keeper, reminding her that the main purpose of her being in the Kingdom at that time could be for the possibility of saving the people. Because of her Jewish heritage, this put Esther in a sensitive position, caught between her loyalty to the King and her desire for the liberation of the Jews.

Mordecai reminded Esther that if she "held her peace," if she "quit" and did not speak her truth at this time, the people would perish. Esther was one among many wives and could only approach the King by invitation, which was the law of the Kingdom. Knowing that she could be killed for breaking the law, Esther nonetheless gathered her strength, put on her finest regalia, and approached the King uninvited. She knew it was her calling to "speak her peace" on behalf of her people.

The King listened carefully and honored the rightness and truth of Esther's plea. He chose to align with Esther instead of his general who was murdering the Jews. A miracle transformation occurred. The King removed the general (who symbolized the old pattern of killing and survival) from command. Mordecai (the faith-keeper and visionary who encouraged Esther to speak) and Esther (who spoke for the new pattern of peace and *thrival*) were both given places of honor in the Kingdom.

Esther could have chosen to quit. Rather than being present to the Spirit of Truth within her, she might easily have chosen to be silent about her Jewish heritage and the plight of her people. Esther, though, did not quit. By saying yes to the Holiest Dream within her, she spoke for peace and kindness and helped save the people.

How can Esther's story apply to the current moment? A lot of us talk about being called. We are called to our work. We are called to take different kinds of action in our lives. If ever there was a time to reflect on your calling or to answer the call more fully, it is now. Like Esther, it may be that the message you bring into the world at this time, along with your actions and presence, can help "save the people."

The hologram of peace lives within every cell and atom of your being. The "holy gram," the holy message, may be that you have "come to the Kingdom for such a time as this" to speak that message, to speak your peace. Your words and your presence make a difference.

Jesus spoke these powerful words recorded in the Gospel of St. Thomas: "If you allow that which is within you to come forward, it will set you free. If you do not allow that which is within you to come forward, it can destroy you."

More than ever, you and I are being invited to answer the call, to bring forth that which is within us, to set ourselves free, to set humanity free.

Jesus also said, "You will do all the things that I have done and greater." Some theologians would like to take a big black magic marker and cross out those words because many of them have not known what to do with that admonition. It is said that Jesus, too, saved the people. You and I are being invited to do all the things that Jesus did and greater, and it is our time—not to quit—but to be present to the Spirit within us, to speak our peace and bring forward truth and kindness.

It is time for us to ask the hard questions and reflect on the very hardest issues. Why does it take an event like 9/11 to stir peoples' massive generosity towards one another? What do countries need? More money and support for the basic needs and well-being of the people, or money for more war weapons? Is it okay to allow people to starve and die from disease and poverty when there is money and technology available in the world to help them? Is it okay to continue paying millions of dollars to make films that have a message of violence and continue to tell the old story of "us against them"? Aren't there more healing stories to be told? Is it okay for some countries and cultures to live with abundance while many people barely have the means to exist? Is it okay for professional athletes and film stars to receive great wealth for their work, while teachers and counselors, who work with children and families, earn such low wages? These are just a few of the hard questions.

It's time for the human family to wake up and make a rigorous recovery from fear to compassion. We've all been participating in the waking-up process for a long time, in many ways, but now it's time to be wide-awake.

David and I had an amazing experience a few years ago when we were invited to do a workshop at a Unity church in California on the theme of "Shifting Into Miracle Thinking." A woman who attended that workshop came to see us for a private counseling and healing session. Her husband was very sick and close to dying. She asked us to accompany her to the hospital and pray with her husband, Bob, that his passing would be one of ease.

Bob had gone into the hospital six weeks earlier for a simple procedure and while there, contracted a staph infection and slipped into a coma. His wife, parents, and children were shocked to hear the doctors' painful news that this young man, age thirty-eight, would be passing within days. The rest of the family was immediately called, and they all gathered at the hospital. With broken hearts they said their good-byes and prepared for the predicted outcome.

Before visiting Bob, David and I met with his wife and the minister of the Unity church in a very sacred place—the hospital parking lot. Any space becomes sacred if you make it so! We joined hands and prayed and asked the two most important questions in these difficult circumstances: "What is it that we most need to know right here and now? and; What does God want us to know in this moment?" We did not focus on past history or what might happen to him in the near future, but only on what was important to know right now.

All four of us were invited to consider this question: "Did Bob's soul want to be released or did he want to physically live and recover?" Even though the doctors saw the probability of this young man dying, we saw the very real possibility that his soul was choosing to stay in the body. We knew that either outcome would be blessed—dying or recovering—but the four of us received the same inner guidance that he wanted to make a rigorous recovery. We were "in one mind and one accord," and standing in the power of faithful agreement as we participated in a ceremony of hands-on healing with Bob. After praying, we whispered to him, "We honor whatever choice you make, and if you choose, you can wake up and recover."

A few days later, the Unity minister contacted us and said that the prayer team at the church also felt guided to pray for Bob to wake up and make a full recovery. The minister asked, "What should I tell them?" David and I responded, "What would Jesus do? We believe he would say 'Go For It!'" And that's just what the prayer team did. A few days later, we received word that Bob had opened his eyes. (Now that doesn't necessarily mean he was out of a coma. If you want to know if someone is awake and present, look into their eyes. Look all the way in. You'll know.) The doctors were then called into the room to examine him. They confirmed that Bob was indeed awake and his family and friends rejoiced!

His wife told us a funny story. During his weeks in a coma when Bob was alone, the nurses kept the TV playing in his room. Interestingly enough, the first thing he did when he came out of the coma was to reach up and turn off the TV! Do you think there's a message there about the awakening process? Miraculously, for the next two years, he made a rigorous recovery, learning to walk, talk, and feed himself again. We actually had the great blessing recently of seeing Bob again when he attended one of our workshops. He's living a much different life than before his illness, not without its challenges, but in his words, "A more mellow, grateful life."

Could Bob have come out of the coma without the prayers and power of agreement? That answer dwells only in the Heart of God. If it is true, though, as quantum physicists are telling us, that outcomes are affected and created by what we're expecting to see, then it was significant that none of us quit seeing the possibility of recovery, even though the doctors did not see this possibility.

We have heard from other people who have also come out of a coma that when they woke up they were different in some way. A shift happened within them. Many of us have been in a kind of spiritual coma—not fully conscious, not fully awake and available to life. The hope is that humankind will very soon wake up and be more fully present to Spirit than they ever have been before.

The poet, Robert Francis, expresses this urgency to be awake and present in his poem, *Summons*.[4]

SUMMONS

Keep me from going to sleep too soon.
Or if I go to sleep too soon,
Come wake me up.
Come any hour of night.
Come whistling up the road.
Stomp on the porch. Bang on the door.
Make me get out of bed and come
And let you in, and light a light.
Tell me the northern lights are on,
And make me look.
Or tell me clouds
Are doing something to the moon
They never did before, and show me.
See that I see.
Talk to me till
I'm half as wide-awake as you,
And start to dress wondering why
I ever went to bed at all.
Tell me the walking is superb.
Not only tell me but persuade me.
You know I'm not too hard persuaded.

The early Bible writers talked about being in the "fullness of God." This means to be fully present in each moment, no matter what it looks like. Living in the fullness of each moment expands our awareness of who we truly are—HUGE spiritual beings.

Ken Carey says it this way in *The Third Millennium*: "There is something huge looking through our eyes."[5] And we can add to that: There is something huge living through us, breathing through us, healing through us, teaching through us—and when we realize this, we bring hope into the world.

What does it take to Live Our Hugeness?

I (Margaret) went to Medjugore in Yugoslavia in 1989, just before the war erupted. I went there to research the apparitions of Mother Mary seen by five visionaries, all children, since 1981. While I was there, I met Father Joso (Joseph), a Catholic priest, whose remarkable story was told in a film by Martin Sheen called "*Gospa*." Through an interpreter Father Joso explained with gentle honesty that his priesthood had only been a profession, not his heart's calling. For many years he had done a good job, but that's what it was—a job. Then the purported apparitions began and his life and work shifted drastically. These five children instigated the change. He said, "If God had told me to choose five children to have this experience, I would not have chosen *these* children! They were not good Catholic children!" (I had to laugh when he said that! There goes God again, shocking us out of our stereotypes!)

Father Joso had no faith in what they were saying and was disgruntled by their stories of seeing "the beautiful lady, the Holy Mother." He did not believe them. Thousands of others did believe the children, however, and were making pilgrimages to Medjugore, crowding the little village with cars and buses, filling the church, and waiting for the hour when the visionaries would see the apparition.

But then the shift happened. He was kneeling in prayer

one day and heard an urgent inner message, "Save the Children!" which he felt came from Mother Mary. He ran to the door of his church, opened it, and saw the five children running frantically through the grape vineyard that surrounded the church, with the Communist police chasing them. He waved the children into the church, hid them, and cared for them for several days until the danger passed. For that choice, he spent eighteen hard, life-threatening months in a Communist prison. While there, an amazing thing happened: his faith deepened and a profound closeness to Holy Spirit developed. His "job" as a priest was transformed to the work of his heart—his calling.

After Father Joso was released from prison, he was transferred to another church. People were drawn to visit him at the new church to receive his healing blessings and prayer. Many miracles occurred in his ministry and he became known as "the healing priest." I was so moved by this story that I decided to visit his church and see him again a few days later. While there, I was fortunate enough to receive his blessing. He prayed for me and did hands-on healing that touched me to the core of my soul. Even though I did not understand his Slavic language, the power of his words and blessing healed a deep wound and I wept for several hours, releasing years and years of grief and sadness.

What did it take for Father Joso to answer *the Call*? Something very hard and difficult. Sometimes that seems to be required. Whatever the circumstances, there is always an invitation to say yes to the Hugeness, the Call of Spirit, the deeper Life within us. God is not confused and Great Mystery is at work in all of it, even in the most difficult of times. *Especially* in these times, say yes to Spirit! The world needs you. You make a difference. Please don't quit!

Did I keep peddling? Yes. During my eighth summer, over many hot Florida days, I learned to ride that old blue bike. As the darkening sky swallowed up the last pink and purple streaks of light, mothers' voices would singsong around the neighborhood, calling children home for dinner. We kids would eke out those last minutes of the day—one more toss of the ball, one more run around the bases, one more game of hopscotch in the street, one more push for me on the bike, and the words I'll always remember, "Keep peddling!"

*Affirmations to help you remember
that your presence is important.*

*Say them everyday, especially
if you feel like quitting.*

Take a deep breath and be in stillness for as long as you choose. Reflect with a quiet pause after you read or say each of these statements:

✧ Holy Spirit is the healer and lives within every cell and atom of my being.

✧ My presence is important.

✧ I choose to dream the holiest dreams.

✧ In each and every moment, I choose to stay present and available to Spirit.

✧ I open to the expansive possibilities of good for myself and for all those I hold in my heart.

✧ Angels and faith-keepers are always available to me.

✧ My prayers are powerful and make a difference.

✧ I dream for peace, hope, and understanding.

✧ I speak my truth with great conviction and I am heard.

✧ I am fully awake. I say yes to Spirit.

✧ I will keep peddling!

GO FOR IT!
BREAKING
THROUGH FEAR

Franklin Roosevelt once said, "The only thing we have to fear is fear itself." Well, there is a lot of fear on the planet right now, especially since 9/11. To face our fears and break through to the other side is one of our greatest challenges. If we don't, it will be very difficult to manifest our dreams and heart's desires. These challenges can literally look and feel like huge walls that stop us right in our tracks.

Margaret and I like to deal with these kinds of fears with a "Face the Fear and Do It Anyway" philosophy. We encourage others to "Go For It!" when a wall appears before them on their path. We also believe there is a higher and holier view that can help us overcome any challenge with great courage, determination, and God-Know-How!

A few years ago, we were facing some difficult issues and fear had us stuck in the muck. We weren't able to see beyond the fear, so we decided to create a powerful Fear Release Workshop that we knew would "move the energy." Together with a couple of friends in Santa Barbara, we devised a "Go For It! Breaking Through Fears Ropes Course" event. You know, one of those fun weekends where you are strapped in and buckled up in harnesses and safety gear and then climb telephone poles forty feet high, stand on tiny ledges, walk across rope bridges, and other challenging maneuvers, yelling, screaming, and cheering each other on.

The idea is to work as a team, supporting each other and moving through the fear one step at a time until completing the obstacle course. With lots of encouragement, everyone succeeded. Everyone was able to negotiate and surmount all of the obstacles, and when we came to the last High Ropes event, we were really pumped up.

To complete the course and get back to the ground, we all had to slide down a 1,000 foot cable which proved to be quite exhilarating, to say the least, and pushed some of us to the limits of our physical and emotional endurance. But each person did it and felt really empowered, excited, and energized. We had conquered the High Ropes!

Ironically, the last event of the workshop was conducted on the ground and proved to be the most challenging of all. This event was called "The Wall." We all stood in front of this twelve-foot sheer, wooden wall, looking at it curiously and listening in disbelief as our mighty Ropes Course leader instructed us to "Get over it." Well, in that moment we all forgot about the great success we had achieved working together as a team throughout the day. We all collapsed into our own thoughts of inadequacy, deciding that it was impossible to get over the wall.

How many times have you faced your walls and made that same decision? The good news is that there is always support from both the seen and the unseen to help us in these situations.

Suddenly, one of the group members had a big "Aha!"

and suggested we pool our ideas and come up with a creative solution to this seemingly impossible task. As soon as we made the decision to continue working as a team, ideas started coming. We shifted into possibility thinking and came up with a plan. The idea was to lift and boost one of the strongest individuals up to the top of the wall. That person could climb over, stand on the ten-foot high ledge that was on the other side of the wall, and be ready to reach down and help the next person get over the top.

Nineteen of the twenty of us supported this idea. However, there was one young, athletic guy whose lifelong program was to do everything by himself and never to count on others for support. He was willing to help the rest of us but then wanted to be the last one to get over the wall without any of our help. He was adamant about this so we honored his decision.

Working together as a team, we lifted and pushed the first person to the top, who then helped from that vantage point to pull the next one up and over. Finally, we all managed to get over the wall and then asked this young man if we could help him, but his programming was too strong and he declined. So, we all watched in amazement as he walked about thirty feet away and said with great determination, "I'm going to run as fast as I can toward the wall, jump up and push off with one foot, boosting myself up as high as I can, and then grab the top and pull myself over."

He obviously thought he was Michael Jordan! But alas, Michael Jordan he was not! He ran toward the wall at full speed, jumped, pushed off, and clawed at the wall as he tried to propel himself up. Unfortunately, he didn't get very far and after slamming into the wall, he fell backwards and hit the ground with a loud thud. Appearing disoriented, he looked up at us rather sheepishly, and once again refusing our help, got up, and walked the thirty feet back for a second try.

We encouraged him to change his mind, but no, stubborn as could be, he took off running as fast as possible, slammed into the wall, fell backwards, bounced off the ground, eyes spinning around, completely embarrassed.

You know the saying, "Three time's a charm." He must have been thinking that, because again he got up, dusted himself off, refused our help, and did the exact same thing for the third time. He hit the wall full force and just ricocheted off it, tumbling around on the ground, dazed and bewildered! When he finally recovered, he looked up at us and in that moment, shift happened! His life changed in the blink of an eye as he asked, "Will you please help me?" For the first time in his life, he asked for support and a lifelong program changed. The group shouted a resounding, "Yes!"

We all put our heads together and came up with a great plan. Three strong people from the top of the wall would hold me upside down by my ankles. I would grab his hands as he jumped up and reached for mine. Then, we would both be pulled up and over the top of the wall. It worked perfectly! Reaching up for help always pays great dividends.

He later told us how powerful it felt to finally let go of all the pressure he constantly put on himself to live his life alone without support. He had never allowed himself to feel vulnerable because to him it was a sign of weakness. But after hitting the wall the third time, some sense literally got knocked into him and he made a decision to change his life. It was just too hard and too lonely to continue doing it the old way. Receiving support actually felt good. The real wall he overcame that day was the belief that he couldn't trust anyone would be there for him. What a shift!

What are your walls and how many times do you run into them before asking for help?

When in fear, we quite often forget to ask some very important questions, such as:

✧ How am I seeing this experience, and how is it affecting me?
✧ Am I trying to figure this out by myself?
✧ What are my support systems, and am I willing to ask for help?
✧ Am I stuck or paralyzed with fear?
✧ Am I breathing?
✧ Do I remember that God is at work in the midst of this experience?
✧ Have I dealt with this kind of experience before? Is this a repeat pattern?
✧ Is this one of my walls?
✧ Are my mind and heart working together to create a solution to this dilemma?

Asking these kinds of questions can shift the focus from being stuck in the fear to freeing the mind and spirit to work together to create a solution and move through the fear. It also reminds us that there are support systems available to help us, both heavenly and Earthly. This makes it so much easier to get over our walls.

We have all had many opportunities to overcome fear. Whenever these fear opportunities arise, there is an important message in the experience that we are being asked to understand. Needless to say, staying in the fear is the greatest obstacle to receiving that message. When we are afraid, everything becomes distorted and we don't see or understand clearly what is truly being presented to us.

Fear is contagious and can spread like wildfire. To put out the flames, it's very important to pause and re-center yourself in order to gain a more holy perspective of what is really happening. Breaking through fear begins in that moment of reflection, because what we are really doing is breaking through a very narrow perspective of tunnel vision into a far more expansive view—the Holy Perspective, the Higher Truth. Seeing more clearly allows our energy to shift and can also affect the energy of others.

Margaret and I were living in Santa Barbara, California, when the Rodney King trial was going on in Los Angeles. The media covered the trial day and night and tension was very high. When the riots began in L.A., fear spread throughout the city, and a lot of people got caught up in it. As fate would have it, we had workshops scheduled on the East Coast and the day the riots started we were on a shuttle bus from Santa Barbara to the Los Angeles airport.

Driving through the "City of Angels" was an amazing experience. Smoke and fires lit up the sky and the sound of gunshots rang through the city. Needless to say, the closer we got to the riots, the more nervous we became. To make matters worse, we could hear news reports of the destruction on the shuttle radio. Well, you guessed it. We got scared and every fearful thought you could imagine was racing through our minds. By the time we finally got to the airport, we were fully immersed in the drama.

When we went into the terminal, we witnessed a scene

right out of a Hollywood disaster movie: Many people were sitting on the floor, some huddled in corners, terrified because it had been reported that snipers were shooting at airplanes. We felt the effects of the chaos rippling through the airport and didn't know what to do. Because of the snipers, air traffic controllers were allowing only one plane to take off every eight minutes. Fear was so thick you could cut it with a knife. So, Margaret and I found our own "safe place" and sat there, dumbfounded and mesmerized by this incredible scene.

Time stood still. I flashed back to Vietnam, to Da Nang during the 1968 Tet offensive. Not a pleasant experience, believe me. I remembered a very scary scene at the Da Nang airport as I was leaving 'Nam. Our plane was taxiing the runway to take off, and rockets were blowing up all around us as the VC tried to take the airport. A scene I'll never forget!

Now, years later, I again felt the fear wanting to take over, so I paused and focused on my breathing. I asked God for help and immediately heard the word "Pray." I felt something huge stirring inside of me, comforting me, and I knew it was God. The feeling of reassurance was far greater than any feeling of fear I'd ever had.

So I looked at Margaret and said, "Let's pray and ask the Divine what this rioting is really all about, what we're supposed to understand from this." She agreed and we took some deep breaths and started praying.

Within a few brief minutes we became calm and felt Divine Presence again. (It's important to remember that fear can cause us to forget about Divine Presence.) We asked God to help us understand what was really happening and both received the same answer, a message that helped us break through our fear and lift our spirits to a new level of understanding.

Both of us stood up at the same time, looked at each other with a renewed sense of peace, and shared our messages. The Divine Message was this: Fear and rage are within us all. People attack others and destroy property only when they are hurting, confused, or oppressed. The people venting their feelings of frustration and taking part in the riots were giving us all an opportunity to look at our own similar unresolved issues. Instead of acting out our anger and frustration on others or beating ourselves up, we can choose to be more compassionate with ourselves and others, and begin to heal those wounds with love and compassion. We all have the capacity to act out our negative thoughts and feelings, but instead of meeting anger with anger, we can shift our thoughts to be more understanding; first toward ourselves for the anger that we carry, then toward the rioters. Love is the healer. Staying in fear only engenders more fear.

Margaret and I knew we had received a powerful healing by asking for the Divine message and making this shift to a more centered place where we could actually hear the answer. From the heart of compassion, we prayed for the rioters as well as their oppressors and sent blessings to everyone involved.

Within five minutes of that prayer, a ticket agent came up to us and said, "We have a plane leaving for Dallas in ten minutes, and we can put you on that plane if you like. Even though Dallas isn't your destination, you can get a connecting flight from there to wherever you want to go." Needless to say, we were grateful for that opportunity!

As you can see, the situation changed dramatically, both an inner change as well as an outer one. The wildfires had been extinguished for us, and we thanked God every minute of that flight to Dallas.

No fear can ever overpower the vast resources of prayer and Divine Thought. Remember, when you take time to reflect on life's fearful experiences instead of reacting to them, you can "see" everything in a whole new light. So pause and pray when fear comes your way, be kind to yourself and ask for higher understanding. There is always a gift when you do. Whatever your destination, fly with God and you will always be safe.

Breaking Through Fear

If fear knocks at your door and walls appear as obstacles on your path, don't panic. Instead, pause, reflect, and turn within for answers. Try some or all of these suggestions to help you to break through the fear and bring the walls tumbling down:

✦ Face the fear as opposed to running from it. Pause, reflect, and remember to breathe, to renew yourself through the breath of God. Breathe this Holy Breath into your heart. God-breath fills you with life force energy and strengthens you, whereas the breath of fear draws life force energy out and weakens you.

✦ Pray and re-center yourself so that the mind and spirit will work together.

✦ Ask for God support as well as support from others who you know will be there for you when you need it.

✦ Remember, God is at work in the midst of this experience—you are not alone.

✦ Ask your inner guidance, "What is this fear all about?" There is always a higher understanding that can provide the answer and ease the fear.

✦ Take positive action to move through the fear as opposed to being paralyzed and stuck in it.

✦ Love is the healer of fear. Remember to nourish yourself with loving, compassionate, healing thoughts.

✦ Ask this question: "Does all of this fear belong to me or

is any of it someone else's fear that I'm feeling? Free yourself from others' fears by sending healing thoughts to them.

✧ Ask for God's blessings and trust you are being held in love.

✧ Remind yourself that no wall and no fear is as powerful as the Divine in your heart. So—Go For It! and break through your fears.

SHIFTING INTO MIRACLE THINKING

We are living in a miraculous time of quantum shifts in human consciousness. Shifting into miracle thinking is an expansion of consciousness that comes from living in our hearts. It is the process that shifts us out of fear, helplessness, and misunderstanding into a powerful wisdom that can create remarkable outcomes in our everyday lives. Some call this "The Awakening," meaning, the realization that we are Divine, that God lives within us, and that we are connected with all that is. Miracle thinking requires us to utilize heart intelligence to glean the wisdom from our life experiences. We are becoming more aware of a higher or deeper source within us that is also present in every life situation. This Presence is bringing forth our ultimate good. The human family is learning to enjoy life rather than just endure it.

"Shift Happens!" We all know this. The big question is: Do we see the shifts in our lives happening for a reason? Do we see God at work, no matter what the moment looks like? How we perceive and interpret what we see is of vital importance! As we move out of the judgmental aspect of ourselves (our ego/mind), with its fear-based perceptions rooted in survival and drama, we move into miracle thinking of the heart.

In our healing ministry, Margaret and I have witnessed numerous healings and miracles throughout the country and have concluded that there are two ingredients present in these exquisite experiences: (1) the God-energy of Love, which is the Healer, and (2) the free, unobstructed flow of this energy moving through the individual, which creates a state of wellness. The Divine generates this energy through the heart.

In every life situation we have an opportunity to flow with the energy of that experience, interact from the heart, and learn what that experience has to teach us. On the other hand, we can make the choice, consciously or unconsciously, to react to the situation by resisting, judging, arguing, or running from it. In the latter case, the consequences of these reactions will more than likely result in not learning what the circumstance has to teach us. Then, an eventual re-creation of a similar experience will be necessary as a new opportunity for learning.

There are two ways to view every situation. They represent the two aspects of self from which we all function. The first aspect of self is the ego, and the second aspect is the heart.

We, as a human race, have struggled to survive for thousands of years. The ego is that part of us that looks at life through the eyes of survival. It is the God-unrealized self that doesn't yet know the truth of who we are. The purpose of our having an ego is to keep us in survival no matter what is happening in our lives. The ego is highly efficient at this skill.

The ego is that aspect of self that doesn't tell the truth (the part of us that is confused, judgmental, and reactionary). The ego sees life through tunnel vision, a very narrow level of perception that distorts our view and understanding of what life presents us. Reaction, as opposed to interaction, is the result of clouded perception and misunderstanding.

When we become reactionary, our lives are filled with lots of drama! I think we are all quite familiar with this aspect of self. Drama keeps us in survival mode and blocks our ability to learn from an experience. Consequently, a new and similar opportunity will come our way to learn this lesson. This process will continue to occur until we actually "get it," gain wisdom, and evolve.

The "survival" energy of the ego functions through various guises, which include fear, separation, judgment, criticism, control, manipulation, protection, and defense. We know each of these well and probably spend a major portion of our lives functioning on one or more of these levels. After all, consider all the survival energy on the planet, the media's dreary portrayal of world events, and the constant change we are dealing with. The more we focus on survival, the more survival dramas we create. It is important to note that certain experiences, like running out of a burning building or jumping out of the way of a car that's about to hit you, involve more of an instinctive survival. I consider instinctive survival to be the heart's discernment to do what is the highest and best for us in the moment.

Most of us have had early childhood experiences that were traumatic. When those situations occurred, the ego convinced us that fear was the only way to get through those circumstances. Knowing that we needed to survive, we turned to the fear-based ego, thinking it would be our safety net. Most of us were not yet aware that God was the true provider of safety and security. We didn't yet know that love was the healer of all wounds. So, as a child, we were not prepared to deal effectively with the dramas and traumas that life presented. Thus, fear cautioned us to listen to the ego and begin the journey of survival.

After living that way for a while, survival energy became familiar to us, so we began to focus more and more on survival and ultimately, began to live from that level of being as if it were the only level. What we focus on is what we get!

For a lot of us, patterns were then established that gave birth to one survival experience after another. Some of these patterns have persisted throughout our lives. In order to shift patterns that are detrimental to our well-being, we must change what we focus on.

It is important to note that throughout our lives, the heart also speaks to us, encouraging a shift in perspective, an embrace of life and learning as opposed to judging and resisting the learning process. This is the holy aspect of self and at some given point in time, most of us make a choice to listen more to the wisdom of the heart. Sometimes that choice is made because we are really "sick and tired of being sick and tired." Sometimes it comes from sheer determination to shift out of survival into thrival.

Survival carries a lot of frustrating energy and constant drama. Most of us become really depleted from this way of existing and want to make a change to flow more easily with each experience. So the heart speaks to us and we begin to listen. As we do, a profound desire grows within us to connect with Spirit.

The heart is that aspect of self that perceives life experiences through a more expansive consciousness. It is the part of us that interacts instead of reacts, flows with the experience, and opens the channels of learning.

The heart functions through one or more of the following responses: love, peace, harmony, embracing, blessing, healing, compassion, forgiveness, joy, divine understanding, and oneness. When we function from the heart, our lives become more meaningful, more productive, and far more God-centered.

The heart is the dreamer of the holiest dream. It is the God-self and its job is to embrace life rather than endure it.

I believe the holiest mission for each of us on the planet is to awaken, to remember the truth of who we are in our hearts, and to live that truth in love consistently. In order to actually accomplish the awakening, we must embrace our life experiences and learn from them, as well as remain nonjudgmental and at peace with the survival needs of the ego.

Ultimately, the goal of the heart is to unify all aspects of self into a oneness of love, so that everything within us works together in harmony. This includes the ego. The more we embrace and understand the experiences of ego and survival, the more we grow and progress on our spiritual path. Then eventually, thrival becomes the more constant pattern from which we live. How we perceive life is a choice. Imagine your life moving along a conveyer belt and in the opposite direction, moving in a constant flow, is one life experience after the next. When each experience reaches you, there is a choice to make: you can react to the experience, go into fight or flight, move into survival and drama, not learn what the experience has to teach you, and then deal with the consequences that this energy affords you. Or, you can interact with the experience, flow with it, embrace the opportunity to learn and grow, and then move on to the next.

I believe we come to this planet to continuously learn and move forward spiritually. God gives us as many opportunities as are necessary to accomplish our goal of learning in this life or as many lifetimes as needed. Earth has proven to be a very interesting place to awaken. On Earth we have numerous experiences and a variety of emotions to deal with. With very few dull moments and constant change our goal remains the same: to live in the truth of our heart no matter what is happening. In order to function more consistently from the heart, we must stop judging and start embracing.

Living in the heart means listening to the Holy Wisdom and following Its guidance to our highest good. When we do this consistently, we don't have to repeat detrimental patterns. We are more stable emotionally and life gets easier. We will always have challenges on this planet, so why not shift into miracle thinking when those challenges come our way?

Each and every one of us has divine guidance, a discerning inner presence that is looking out for us. Our heart is the holy, universal connection with all of life. It is God within! I have learned through a variety of life experiences to perceive the difference between my heart's wisdom and my egoic needs. On many occasions when I have listened to this impeccable guidance, I have been led on a path that illuminated my life with miracles.

The following is a true story of how my heart wisdom led me on a miracle path that changed my life in a profound way:

In 1985, I dreamed of a change I wanted to make in my life. I was living in Daytona Beach, Florida, but really wanted to live in California and in particular, Santa Barbara, even though I didn't know anyone there. I had wanted this for a long time but was not doing anything to manifest my dream. Have you noticed that when you don't take any appropriate action, the Divine will sometimes give you a quantum boost to urge you forward toward your heart's desire?

One morning I was awakened from a deep sleep to the sound of an inner voice that spoke clearly and distinctly saying, "Pack your bags, get in your car, and drive to Santa Barbara." Wow! What a message! You know how we like to argue with that voice? Well, I did—for several hours—but the message continued and got stronger as the day went on. So, I decided to sit down, clear my mind, and pray to see if this was truly the best thing for me to do. Within minutes my prayers were answered with a resounding "Yes, Go For It!"

Believe it or not, I packed my bags that day and started the drive to Santa Barbara. It's true that I am a risk-taker, and I know that taking a risk is sometimes necessary to create a powerful shift in your life. It took four days to get to Santa Barbara and when I arrived, I pulled up to a Motel 6 near the beach. I went into my room, unpacked my bags and decided to take in my new surroundings. As I looked around, I thought to myself, *Oh my God, what am I going to do now?* I didn't have a clue. I didn't know anyone, didn't have a job, and didn't know where to start.

Out of the blue, that inner voice spoke to me again and said, *Open the phone book, close your eyes and touch someone's name, then call them and introduce yourself.* Whoa! You can imagine what I thought of that idea! But I figured since I was in California now, anything goes, so I said, "What the heck, I'm going for it."

Now remember, this is a true story. I opened the phone

book, closed my eyes and touched someone's name. It happened to be a woman's name, so I held my breath and prayed I would get her answering machine, but no, she answered the phone. I took another deep breath and told her my story of arriving in California that very day and listening to the inner guidance to call someone and introduce myself. Believing she probably thought I was from never-never land, I waited anxiously for her response.

She said, "Dave, I'm so glad you called! I'm a facilitator of a personal growth workshop that is happening this weekend, and there will be over a hundred people there, many of whom are healers, counselors, and teachers. So you must come to the workshop. I know wonderful things will happen for you!"

I was flabbergasted and said, "I'll be there!"

During the workshop I had a chance to stand before the group and tell my story. After I did, 120 people stood up and clapped and said "Welcome home, Dave." I felt so accepted and knew that this was the right place for me. Not only did I meet some exceptional people that day, but I also got a position as a counselor in Santa Barbara and a place to stay in someone's home until I got established.

Why did this miracle shift happen? Because I dreamed of positive change in my life, listened to the inner voice guiding me, prayed and asked for heart wisdom to make the best decision, and then received a resounding, "Go For It." I felt sure it was God-guidance because I experienced great joy and excitement and had a sense of "knowing" that it was right for me. (Ever know that you just know something?) And then I took action. I went for it and my dream came true—a new life with new surroundings in beautiful Santa

Barbara, new friends, and most of all an even stronger belief in miracles.

Remember, shift happens! Why not make your shifts miracle shifts? Listen to your heart's wisdom and embrace life's experiences. There's a reason for everything, and our heart guides us on the path of life's exceptional learning. So be at peace with who you truly are, and know that your life thrives when God-directed.

Shifting from the Head to the Heart

This technique is a three-step process to help shift out of an egoic perspective and into the heart perspective. The shift offers us an opportunity to learn from the experience. This process can be used whenever you have an egoic thought or circumstance and can be highly effective in shifting the outcome of the experience from reactive drama to a much more positive and healing interaction.

I learned this technique some time ago, have practiced it with exceptional results, and have taught it to hundreds of people over the years. I have heard from a lot of these people that the "Shifting From the Head to the Heart" process enabled them to live a more positive, productive life. Practice this three-step process every day:

1. *Choose the Heart.* Whenever you have an egoic thought or experience (fear, survival, separation, judgment, criticism, control, manipulation, protection, or defense), instead of reacting, simply pause for a moment and observe the experience without judgment as if you were looking at a movie.

You're the star of this movie and for the sake of this exercise, let's say fear is the experience you're having. Fear is one of the most paralyzing, overpowering functions of the ego. As you observe, take note that you are now in fear, and since that is a function of the ego, you must therefore be reacting from the ego at this present time.

You now have a choice. You can react to the fear and delve

into the drama of survival energy, or you can make a decision to move that energy into your heart. Knowing you have this choice, instead of just reacting, is very empowering.

To make that quantum leap, consciously say that you want to be in heart energy, then send yourself a heart blessing—a loving embrace of energy, healing words, or holy thoughts that surround you and comfort the feelings of fear.

Here's an example of what I'm talking about. Whenever I'm afraid, I imagine myself being held and comforted in the arms of angels. I have a great love for angels, so this immediately shifts my focus from fear to comfort, love, and blessings, and that begins the process of moving the energy into my heart. Only the heart knows how to bless!

So, the first step is to observe your experience without judgment, determine if your experience is ego-based, and if so, choose to be in your heart by sending yourself a blessing, thereby embracing and accepting whichever egoic function you are experiencing.

2. *Make the Calls.* Call forth the Holy Spirit to move the energy and perception of your experience out of the ego and into the heart. Calling forth the Holy Spirit is a powerful way I have found to ensure a more positive and consistent way of living in Divine Spirit energy. Invoking Christ energy in our thoughts, words, and actions helps us function from a holy place, which in turn helps the awakening process to unfold more creatively in every life experience.

Calling on the power of the Holy Spirit is a powerful and highly effective way to still the mind and expand the heart. When we call forth this energy into our heart, we create a gentle flow of God-essence that provides peace, harmony, love, courage, and healing.

Making the calls to Divine Spirit can be used to overcome detrimental thought patterns, to gain high perspective
of life's experiences, to transform fear, and to provide positive energy for our dreams. The Holy Spirit is the
miraculous energy that helps us create remarkable outcomes. So, sit quietly, take a deep God-breath and read
silently to yourself or say out loud the following invocation:

✧ I call forth the infilling of the Divine Light of the Christ
(or the names of your Beloved Holy Ones).

✧ I call forth a perfect circle of light and love to surround
me.

✧ I call forth the holy healing breath of God to breathe
within me.

✧ I call forth the power of the Holy Spirit to move through
me now, to gently flow into my heart, to bathe my heart
in the power of love.

✧ I now call on that sweet spirit to pour forth from my
heart like a river of healing light, touching each and
every cell, renewing, restoring, and regenerating as it
moves through me and around me in a halo of healing
light, immersed in the holy energy, blessed in love. Now,
direct that flow of energy to move from your heart
throughout your entire being and then surround you in
a halo of healing light.

Why do we call on the Holy Spirit? Because it is the most
powerful energy of the universe, far more powerful than any
egoic thought or circumstance. When you call on Holy
Spirit, Shift Happens! Once you have filled your heart and
your being with Divine Spirit, a calmness and a feeling of

centeredness occurs. You can then become more present in the moment and peaceful in the Holy Energy instead of remaining upset in fear.

3. *Interact With Love.* From the heartfelt centeredness that Holy Spirit provides, you can now interact with the experience, coming from love, peace, and harmony, as opposed to reacting from fear, judgment, or survival. What do you suppose will happen to the outcome of the experience when you make this shift?

Heart interaction creates clear communication, gentle flowing energy, possibilities for learning, and positive, creative outcomes. You won't be debilitated by the fear because the heart knows no fear, only love. Love is the healer of fear. Every time you complete this process, there is one more moment of love in your life and one less moment of fear.

Practice the three-step process every day or whenever you have an egoic experience. This will increase the love energy in your life.

Make the calls to invoke the Divine Energy into your heart when you wake up in the morning, before going to sleep at night, before you pray and meditate, and whenever you have an important choice, interaction, or decision to make. This ensures that you are being guided by love. So, make friends with your ego, give it a hug, do lunch with it! It's all a part of shifting into miracle thinking. May all your shifts be miracles ones!

Compassion and Forgiveness—
Pathways to
Higher Ground

The sage asks, "Did I dream the butterfly or did the butterfly dream me?" Are we daring to create dreams or is Big Dream living and creating through us? It is both. David says, "We are all God's dream come true." We live in the field of creative energy that quantum physicists explain, and we *are* the field. If Big Dream is living through us, as us, what is the creative intention of that life energy? I believe it is the continual evolution of humankind. The evolution of compassionate consciousness toward all peoples, nations, our Earth, all life—the four leggeds, the winged ones, the mineral people, the tree people, the creepy and crawly ones—all beings, all life.

Humankind's dreams are aspects of the One Great Dream. Created as magnificent spiritual beings with many facets of body, mind, and emotions, we contain and express elements of all the dreams that have ever been dreamt, all the joys, all the sorrows, all the tragedies, all the triumphs. The One Great Dream—Universal Mind, God, Spirit—is pulling and urging us towards higher expression of our own magnificence, moving us forward and deeper into the evolving and emerging consciousness of compassion and forgiveness where truly inspired dreams are born.

The human family has made many choices based on fear and those choices have created more fear. As we evolve, we become more aware of where our dreams and actions are birthed, either in the womb of fear or the womb of love. Choosing higher ground elevates and allows us to create with the spirit of love for ourselves, our loved ones, the children, the Earth, and on and on. An old gospel song about higher ground goes like this:

> *Lord lift me up and let me stand*
> *by faith on Heaven's table land.*
> *A higher plane than I have found,*
> *Lord plant my feet on Higher Ground.*
> *I have no desire to stay where doubts*
> *arise and fears dismay.*
> *Though some may dwell*
> *where these abound,*
> *my prayer, my aim, is Higher Ground.*

The Great Plains Indians tell a story about "Jumping Mouse," which I first read in Hyemeyohsts Storm's book *Seven Arrows.*[6] His longer rendition is rich with insight and teaching, but briefly, the story goes like this:

Once there was a mouse who kept his nose to the ground and stayed very busy doing mouse things. Now and then he heard a strange, roaring sound and lifted his head to see what it was, asking his mouse friends, "What is that sound?" But they didn't hear the sound and went back to doing their chores. Mouse remained curious and when he heard the roaring sound again, he decided to go and investigate.

He met a raccoon along the way who said, "Little Brother, the sound you hear is the River. Come on, I'll show you." Mouse had never seen a river and was afraid, but he followed Raccoon and saw that the river was a great and mighty thing, full of life and powerful energy. At the river's edge Raccoon said, "I have to leave now, but I want you to meet my friend, Frog." Frog was in the river and Mouse asked him, "Aren't you afraid to be so far out in the Great River?" Frog answered that he had the gift, the "medicine," of living both in and out of the river. Frog told Mouse that he, too, could have powerful medicine if he would crouch really low and then jump as high as he could.

Mouse crouched low, then jumped as high as he was able, and when he did, Little Mouse saw something incredible. He could hardly believe such a thing existed, something so different from his world on the low ground! Then, when he landed, he fell in the river! He was wet and afraid and angry with Frog for tricking him. Frog said, "Wait a minute. You're not hurt, just wet. Don't let your fear and anger blind you! What did you see?" Mouse thought for a moment and said, "I saw the Sacred Mountains." Then Frog gave Mouse a new name, "Jumping Mouse," which made him very happy.

Jumping Mouse returned to his mouse world and very excitedly told his friends about the Great River and the Sacred Mountains, but no one believed him. They didn't like him because he seemed different now. His friends noticed he was wet and yet there had been no rain. They didn't understand this mystery and were afraid of him. Jumping Mouse felt alone and hurt. However, he knew they couldn't understand. How could they? They didn't know what he knew because they had never seen anything but the low ground. He had heard the Great River and had even been immersed in it. He had bent down low and jumped up high and seen the Sacred Mountains.

So, one day Jumping Mouse left his mouse world and set off in another direction. He came to a great, vast prairie that appeared to go on forever. He knew it had to be crossed to get to the Sacred Mountains. There were eagles circling overhead, and he was very afraid, but he set off running from one sage bush to another. In the shade of one of the sage bushes, he met an old mouse who had lived in the desert for many years. "Yes," Sage Mouse said, "I've learned to live safely here among the protective bushes and to stay low when the eagles are too near. Forget about the Sacred Mountains, they are only a myth. Stay here with me. It is a good place to live. There's plenty of food on the edge of the prairie."

Jumping Mouse decided to stay with Sage Mouse for a while, and they lived in the shade under the bushes where there was plenty of food and a feeling of safety. But he couldn't forget the Sacred Mountains and was determined to cross the prairie and make his way to them.

The day came when he felt ready, so with a little, pounding, mouse heart, he set off running as fast as he could. He could see the eagles flying closer, so he ran for a chokecherry bush and hid there in the cool shade, eating cherries and grass seeds. He stayed there quite a long time, safely eating, even getting a little lazy and a little forgetful about his dream of reaching the Sacred Mountains.

Then one day he was awakened from his nap by the sound of heavy breathing and discovered a great buffalo with huge black horns, lying near the chokecherry bush. Jumping Mouse asked, "Great Buffalo, why are you lying here at the edge of the prairie?" "I am dying," said Great Buffalo, "and my Medicine told me that only the Eye of a mouse can heal me. But I don't believe in such a thing. I've never seen a mouse on the prairie."

Jumping Mouse was afraid. *One of my eyes!* he thought, *but he will die if I don't give him an eye, and it is a shame to let such a Great Being die.* So, he went to the buffalo who lay dying and said, "I am Jumping Mouse and I have two eyes. You may have one of them." With this gift of compassion, Buffalo was made whole. He stood up, strong and powerful, and said, "Thank you, little brother. I know about your visit to the Great River and your quest for the Sacred Mountains. You have given me life so that I may give life to the People. I will now help you cross the Great Prairie." So, Jumping Mouse ran on the ground, hidden beneath the belly of the Great Buffalo who moved confidently across the prairie. Eagles flew overhead but all they could see below was the magnificent, powerful buffalo.

When they got across the prairie, the two friends parted and Jumping Mouse met a wolf who was just sitting lazily, doing nothing. When Jumping Mouse said, "Hello, Wolf," it seemed to stir something within this great being and he said "Oh yes, that's who I am, a wolf!" You see, Wolf had lost his memory and forgotten his greatness. This made Jumping Mouse sad, and he thought for a long time about what he could do to help this great being. Then he remembered how Great Buffalo had been healed and he gave the wolf the same medicine, his one remaining eye. "You are a true brother," Wolf said. "Both of your mouse eyes are gone, but don't worry, you have given me back my memory, and I am the Guide to the Sacred Mountains. I will take you there." Great Wolf guided Jumping Mouse through the forest to the Sacred Mountains and Medicine Lake where Jumping Mouse drank the refreshing, clear water.

Great Wolf left and Jumping Mouse got scared and started trembling. He felt alone and knew that the eagles would certainly find him now. He lamented, "Why did I give my eyes away. Now I'm alone and blind!" Jumping Mouse sat by Medicine Lake, drinking more of the clear water amongst the Sacred Mountains. Then it became clear to him: For the "give away" of his first eye to his friend, Great Buffalo, Jumping Mouse received the gift of being protected as he crossed the prairie. And for the "give away" of his second eye to his friend, Great Wolf, Jumping Mouse was given the gift of being guided to the Sacred Mountains. And now he understood that his life journey would continue with Great Eagle who would surely come for him. When Great Eagle did come, Jumping Mouse heard the eagle call and felt a shadow on his back. There was a bright flash of light that filled his mind and Jumping Mouse fell asleep.

Then he awoke and was surprised to still be alive! And, he could see! There were many beautiful colors, but shapes were blurry. Then he heard a voice that said, "Hello, Brother. Do you want some Medicine?" "Yes!" said Jumping Mouse. "Then crouch down very low and jump as high as you can," the voice instructed. He bent low, then jumped high, and the wind carried him higher and higher. "Don't be afraid. Trust the wind!" said the Voice. When Jumping Mouse opened his eyes again, he could see clearly, and the higher he went, the clearer and farther he could see. Soaring high, he looked down and saw his old friend, Frog, by the river. Frog looked up at his friend soaring high above the river and called out loudly, "You now have a new name!" Jumping Mouse listened carefully and heard Frog shout, "You are Eagle!"

We, too, are making our way toward the higher vantage point of true SELF—"Serving Eternal Life Force"—where we know our true name, our true nature, and can see more clearly; ". . . with our unveiled faces reflecting like mirrors the Glory of the Lord, [while] all grows brighter and brighter as we are turned into the image that we reflect." (I Corinthians 3:18)

Jumping Mouse was on his journey of awakening just as we are. He was afraid, sometimes confused, and tempted to stay in the safety of his mouse friends or lazily eat the chokecherries. He had to think hard about his "give aways," and it would have been understandable for him to be afraid of Buffalo and Wolf, but they became his allies. And, of course, the one he was most afraid of was Eagle, who became his greatest creative force. He had the choice all along to say no to Great Dream. When we say no and keep ourselves away from the Great River and Sacred Mountains, we deprive ourselves of our source of creativity, our inspiration, and our compassionate connection with self and others. Then, it feels as if we lose our higher ground and disconnect from Spirit.

David and I taught a university class entitled "Spirituality, Psychology, and Healing" in which we asked the question, "When you feel you've disconnected from your spiritual self, God, or Spirit, how do you reconnect?" Everyone in the class had really interesting and informative suggestions like prayer, meditation, walking in nature, yoga, reading inspirational books, listening to music, dance, art, spending time with their children or grandparents—all good and helpful ideas.

One individual, a Klamath Indian man, did not speak, so I asked him directly, "How do you reconnect with Spirit?" He took a few moments before speaking, and then respectfully said, "I don't disconnect." It was not even in his frame of reference that it was possible to disconnect. And of course he's absolutely right! It just *seems* like we disconnect.

The poet, Kabir, writes, "We are like thirsty fish, swimming in the water." Teeming life energy is all around and within us. Jesus called it "The River of Life." This renewing, restorative, regenerative "Medicine Lake" empowers the soul, clears the mind, and tunes our awareness to the Holy Dream. "Aha" insights, and the informing details and connecting pieces of the Dream come more easily into our awareness. We pay more attention to the "teachers" and "healers" that surround us—all of nature, the birds and the wind, the voices that speak to us in both our sleeping and waking dreams, the heavenly embrace that supports, heals and restores our "eyes to see and ears to hear"—and all of the rich creative energy that surrounds, enriches, and lifts us.

From this higher ground we are inspired to create holy dreams, to heal, and to restore our souls through the way we interpret circumstances, the way we view ourselves and others, *and* the way we forgive. Where there are old wounds and hatred, there is also a growing understanding of self and others, nations and religions, individuals and organizations—and God. Ultimately, if we are willing, we can achieve one of the greatest demonstrations of love and kindness possible—genuine forgiveness. We can compassionately release our own souls and the souls of others from the grip of hatred, prejudice, misperceptions, and all the other harmful thoughts and actions humans have perpetrated upon one another.

The pathways of genuine forgiveness and compassion open us to live in the Great Field of Possibilities, and to manifest our dreams from that space of creative life energy that exists within us and around us—the Great Mystery. Mapping our direction on these two pathways helps us to let go of old ways of perceiving and move to a higher, more evolved way of seeing with the same Christ Mind (Christ meaning "Anointed"). The same Christ Consciousness that Jesus demonstrated when he looked down from the cross and prayed for his executioners: "Father, forgive them, for they know not what they do!"

Forgiveness, the giving of your compassion, can seem like an impossible choice, especially when you have been badly hurt or betrayed. It is comforting to know that it is not always necessary to demonstrate this huge act of kindness by yourself. If it feels too hard to genuinely forgive those who have hurt you, look how Jesus did it. He said "*Father*, forgive them." In other words "Father, you do it! I can't do this alone." Metaphysically, I interpret these powerful words of the Christ in this way:

Father, *High Consciousness, Eternal Omnipotent Consciousness of Love that knows and understands all things,* **Forgive them, for they know not what they do.** *Give unto them life and understanding and bring them to High Holy Wisdom. Forgive this debt. Release their souls* *unto Life rather than forgetfulness. Set their souls free from the weight of this unconscious act, because they are in pain and afraid. They do not know the presence of Love, the presence of Healing, the high, holy Consciousness that is in their midst. They do not yet have the "ears to hear and the eyes to see." They do not recognize the Heart of Love within themselves, so how can they recognize it in me, the Christ? Forgive them, for they do not understand this mystery and have chosen to destroy what they do not understand.*

There is a story about the Buddha whose countenance was so lighted up that when he walked through a town, people would stop him and ask, "Are you an angel?"

"No," the Buddha would reply.

"Are you a holy one?" they would then ask.

Again he would answer, "No."

"Then tell us who you are," the people demanded.

The Buddha replied, "I am awake."

We all have an opportunity to be more awake, to be more "light" even where there is fear and misunderstanding. Genuine forgiveness is a quality of awakened perspective that can release us, as well as others, from further harm. Forgiveness is the only choice when one is truly awake. In this expanded awareness, we see with clearer vision our own actions and the actions of those with whom we've shared the journey.

How do we truly allow compassion and genuine forgiveness to live in our hearts? How do we even consider that it's possible?

Remember the story about the angry crowd who asked Jesus to pass judgment on a woman prostitute who had broken the law by committing adultery? The law stated that she must be stoned. Now, stoning was not just tossing some pebbles at the accused. Stoning meant that huge rocks were piled on top of a human being until there was no breath left in their body. This woman had reason to be afraid! Her accusers were yelling, "Stone her!" and the angry Jewish men were testing Jesus by asking him to be her judge. You see, Jesus had broken some Jewish laws himself, one of which was welcoming women to learn about the scriptures and to participate in the New Way he was proclaiming.

Jesus demonstrated a powerful shift when he asked for a higher, holy perspective and opened to the vast field of possibilities within Spirit. It was reported that his first action was to pause, then breathe, and I'm sure he was inwardly asking for guidance and heavenly support. He knelt on the ground and the scriptures say he wrote something in the sand. I don't know what he wrote. With this terrified woman standing by his side, maybe he wrote "Breathe!" Maybe he made the sign of the fish, an important symbol for Jesus and his disciples. Or, maybe he just did a Divine Doodle! I don't know. It could be that he was taking time to pray and tune into higher wisdom of Spirit to ask, "What is the highest and holiest response that will release these souls from harm at this time?"

You remember what he did next? He admonished the angry men, saying, "You who have never broken the law, cast the first stone."

Whenever I meditate on this story, I imagine this: After speaking, Jesus again knelt and continued to "doodle." Imagine the SILENCE as his statement pierced and reached the core of Truth in each man's heart. No man was without sin (breaking laws, missing the mark, forgetting one's true self). Stones dropped from clenched fists, and men left the scene one by one, heads bowed. There would be no execution on this day! Only Jesus and the woman remained in that quiet, still place.

Jesus then turned to the woman and said (I am paraphrasing), "Your accusers have gone. Now go and know that the love you seek is within your own heart. Stop looking for love from these men who want only your body. Love yourself wholly, honor yourself as holy and sacred. God sees the beauty of your life even though you have forgotten, and God will hold this knowing for you until you remember. Now go and know you are truly loved."

That's where the story ended in scripture. However, it kept going in my meditation, and I offer this continuing story for your consideration:

The woman left and only Jesus was standing in that place where truth had been spoken. Stones lay scattered on the ground, each one marking the place where minutes before a man had stood, ready to kill. Jesus carefully lifted a stone, held it lovingly in his hands, and sent blessings from his heart to the heart of the one who had held it before him. "Blessings to you and all your generations. Thank you for making another choice. Thank you for following the higher law." Then he lovingly placed the stone on the ground where the woman had stood. He performed this ceremony with each stone and placed them one upon the other, building an altar similar to those in rural Mexico or Ireland that honor the saints, Jesus or Mary; or like the shrines that mark holy sites, sacred wells, and places where miracles have happened; or a place where someone has died to mark the releasing of the soul.

A miracle happened that day. One among them, Jesus, chose to "give away" compassion. He chose to forgive the woman as well as the men with whom she had broken the law. A SHIFT happened. Jesus invited these men to make another choice, to rise to a place of seeing more clearly, to be in truth and see their own part in "breaking the law." We've all broken the "law," either the laws of our society, culture, or religion, laws within our families, laws we established for ourselves, and laws of universal Love. Each one of us is invited to drop our stones of fear, anger, and hatred as many times as is necessary, and make the compassionate choice that creates healing and soul renewal for as many as possible.

John Beeson wrote in his 1859 treatise, *Plea for the Indians,* "The power to do good involves the responsibility of doing it!"[7] The work of forgiveness—forgiveness toward anyone or anything that feels like a "breaking the law" experience—is a holy responsibility. *Forgiveness does not mean that you condone or accept the act.* But it *does* mean you see from higher perspective how every experience is a part of the holy fabric that weaves the journey and evolves the Great Dream.

High Holy Wisdom invites us all to let go of our stones. What a relief to stop hauling them around! I for one am tired of carrying those stones! Better to build an altar to mark my journey where healing shifts have happened. Like that great old African American Gospel, "Gonna lay down my burdens, down by the riverside. I ain't gonna study war no more."

Our choice to forgive crumbles the "Berlin Walls" of fear, anger, depression, and disconnection from our holy dream. Floodgates begin to open and rich, living waters of creativity, enthusiasm, and direction begin to move into the parched, cracked riverbeds. Life returns to the river and the river-banks. It is the life force that Hildegard of Bingen spoke of when she wrote that humanity is "showered with greening refreshment, the vitality to bear fruit," the greening that renews, invigorates, restores, and delivers us unto life as we were created to live it—magnificently.

Altar Stone Meditation

I invite you to read the following meditation and reflectively consider each part of the story about Jesus, the woman, and the angry crowd. In a quiet, still place, close your eyes, take some deep holy breaths, and pause just as Jesus did. Become still.

- ✧ Think of a time when you felt very afraid. Breathe and pause. Now place yourself in the mind and emotions of the woman. How must she have felt? Heart racing, facing certain death, terrified, ashamed. Have you ever been accused of "breaking the law"—anyone's law? Rightly or wrongly accused? The feelings can be anguishing, and the energy launched by others can be a "killing" energy. What do you feel as you connect with the mind and soul of this woman? Pause and reflect on her experience.

- ✧ When complete, pause. Breathe. And place yourself in the mind and emotions of the angry men. How must they have felt? Imagine them full of self-righteous anger, hostility and mob consciousness, acting out those behaviors without thinking about the consequences. Ever been that angry? Angry enough to think about pulling a trigger or hurling a stone, or angry enough to actually do it? Have you ever felt justified to hurl that stone? Have you ever wished yourself or someone else dead? Have you hurled powerful thoughts at yourself or others who you believed had "broken a law"? What do you feel as you connect with the minds and souls of these men? Pause and reflect on their experience.

✧ Now, pause. Breathe. And place yourself in the mind and soul of the Holy One, Jesus, who spoke truth and love into a moment of madness. The holy teacher who spoke sanity into a moment of insanity, calling forth a sense of humanity, urging the crowd to be human. Sometimes we say "Well, I'm ONLY human!" What if we said, "Well, I am human." What does human mean? In Sanskrit, "Hu" means "God," so human means God and Man together—Humankind with God Heart.

✧ Imagine what Jesus felt in that moment. Have you ever been inspired to speak as "the holy one," to speak in a way that can be heard by "the angry consciousness," your own or someone else's? Remember how that felt—heart pounding or with a sense of peace—speaking truth into a moment of insanity. Pause and reflect on Jesus' experience.

You see, most of us have experienced each kind of consciousness: the terrified woman accused of breaking the law; the angry crowd, feeling self-righteous and justified by the law to harm or "kill"; and the wise compassionate teacher. No matter what the situation is, we always have the choice to be in the role of wise teacher. We can speak the truth, see things clearly, judge wisely the course of right action, and rise into God-centeredness in a world that in many ways appears to be insane. A world that is weeping and wailing for healing, and waiting for the manifestation of those who live by the higher laws of love, compassion, and forgiveness.

✧ Think of the stones in your life that you have wanted to throw at someone, some group, an institution, or even yourself.

✧ Pause. Breathe. And from your heart, decide whether you choose to build an altar with the stones or do harm with the stones.

✧ Pause. Breathe. Reflect. See your life journey. It has taken you to many places, brought you many experiences and opportunities for remembering yourself as an eternal spiritual being. See all those places where you picked up stones to throw or felt that stones were being thrown at you.

✧ Pause, breathe. Now, from the perspective of your heart imagination, go to each place. Pause. Pray. And decide whether you will bless or harm with the stones. If you choose blessing, you can then build an altar with them. You can drop all the stones at once, or you can release them one by one as you are ready. Each altar you build marks a holy place, a place where a shift in your consciousness has occurred.

Perhaps when you're finished, the healing still doesn't feel complete. In that case the altar marks a place where healing *is beginning or continuing to happen.* It is in process.

We all have many opportunities to build altars along the way in our holy journey to higher ground. May you travel with peace and may the Wise Teacher within guide and bless your dreams.

THE HEALING
DREAM IN
EVERY STORY

"Oh God," the elder Rabbi prayed, "help me remember the *truth* about myself, no matter how *beautiful* it is!" His eyes twinkled and a satisfied grin swept across his wrinkled face. His audience shook with tickling waves of laughter as awareness crept over their smiling faces.

Seeing beauty in ourselves and in others and in all life is one of the great healing journeys of the soul. Through dark and lighted places, the adventure is profoundly enriched when we consider this: All things work together and the healing dream is ever unfolding for the good. No matter what the situation looks like, whether joyful or painful, possibilities for good, beauty, and healing are embedded in every life story.

In *The Way of the Wizard,* Deepak Chopra says, "Your eye is the life giver of everything it sees."[8] The stories we tell about ourselves, others, our circumstances, and the meaning we give to those stories, either enlivens or diminishes, heals or harms. The way we view the world and ourselves in the world can create healing outcomes—or not.

There is a story about a man who lived in France in the

mid 1800's. Times were hard and his family, like many others, had nowhere to live except cold, dirty alleyways. Jobs were scarce and his children were starving, so he made the desperate decision to steal food for his family. Sadly, during the robbery a shopkeeper was killed. The man's only intention had been to get food for his children, not to kill anyone, but for this crime he was sentenced to life in prison.

After many tortured years of back-breaking labor, he made another life-changing decision: he escaped from prison. Afraid, alone, and once again starving, he ran for his life, exhaustingly trekking through mountain passes and across rivers. Finally, he was far enough away from the prison to stop for rest and hide in a big stone barn. Cold and hungry, weariness overtook him and he slept for days.

A week passed when one day the farmer's young grandchildren were playing in the barn and heard snoring in the hayloft. They quietly climbed the ladder and discovered the convict in torn, dirty clothes, sleeping huddled and shivering under the hay. Soon he awoke from his fitful sleep, surrounded by the three, small children who were curiously and quietly watching him. They were trusting and innocent, not inquiring who he was or where he had come from, but, as young children often do, simply asking, "Will you tell us a story?"

Cautiously, he considered the children's request and consented to tell the only stories he knew, which were Bible stories that he had heard as a boy from his grandmother. So, each day the children would secretly visit the man in the barn. They brought soap and water, warm clothes and blankets, and they always asked for stories. Because he spoke so much of God, the children reasoned that this long-haired, bearded man must be Jesus. Filled with faith, as young children often are, they asked him to pray for their beloved grandfather who had been sick for weeks and was most probably dying.

The convict awkwardly knelt as he had seen his grandmother do so many times. Lifting his eyes toward the sky and folding his hands, the former prisoner whispered a tender prayer for the farmer whose barn had become his safe haven. As he prayed, the children watched his face soften with a glowing, ethereal light. By the time he said "Amen," tears filled his eyes and the same soft light filled the hayloft.

A few days later the children raced to the barn and hurriedly climbed the ladder to the loft. Laughing ecstatically, they announced that family and neighbors were baffled with this turn of events and happily celebrating their grandfather's remarkable recovery! The old farmer himself was most surprised of all and was on his way to the barn to meet this man of miracles for the first time.

If the farmer had seen the convict weeks before, he would have seen in his face a much different story. Years of grueling hard labor had taken its toll, though the suffering of losing his family was even harder. Now the man was clean, well nourished, rested, and inexplicably peaceful, beyond even his own understanding.

As he timidly approached the man whom the children called Jesus, the grandfather's eyes filled with tears because he gazed upon the most gentle face he'd ever seen, one that mysteriously glowed with an otherworldly light. Leaning on his grandchildren's shoulders for support, the farmer struggled to kneel and then humbly asked forgiveness from "Jesus" for a life lived with such inconstant faith. The convict gently rested his hand on the farmer's head and whispered, "You are forgiven, my good and faithful servant." Gradually, a quiet stillness permeated the hayloft sanctuary as the children knelt in prayer beside their grandfather. After a long prayerful silence the farmer gratefully opened his tear-filled eyes and discovered that the man of God was no longer standing beside him. No one saw or heard him leave. No other villagers saw him walking through their fields or sleeping in their barns, and it is said that from that day forward he was never seen again. Yet all these years later the beloved story continues to be told of the man who some say was Jesus.

Our hearts lead us to ask these healing questions: What if the children had perceived just a dirty, starving convict? What if, to them as well as to their grandfather, he had remained only that? To allow the healing dream to come forward we must look beyond the outer appearance to the good unfolding. This way we can see meaning, sense redeeming grace, and even witness transformation.

Harold Goddard says: "The destiny of the world is determined less by the battles that are lost and won than by the stories it loves and believes in." Humankind, especially in Western culture, has many stories of battles won and lost. We have always looked for clear outcomes of winners and losers, good and bad, victory or loss. But when we look deeper into our stories and see beyond the "enemy," then what we fear or do not understand is transformed. We are transformed. And true victory is found.

When we see our stories with healing eyes, there is blessing for everyone. What *is* healing? In her book, *Woman as Healer*, Jeanne Achterberg gives "Eight Concepts of

Healing."⁹ You may want to expand this list for your own definition of healing. Consider that this renewing energy is available in every life experience.

1. Healing is a lifelong journey toward wholeness.
2. Healing is remembering what has been forgotten about connection, unity, and interdependence among all things living and nonliving.
3. Healing is embracing what is most feared.
4. Healing is opening what has been closed, softening what has hardened into obstruction.
5. Healing is entering into the transcendent, timeless moment when one experiences the Divine.
6. Healing is creativity and passion and love.
7. Healing is seeking and expressing self in its fullness, its light and shadow, its male and female.
8. Healing is learning to trust life.

David and I once facilitated a workshop for a group of healers, including nurses, psychotherapists, body workers, clergy, and medical doctors. We made this suggestion to the group: "Honor all that you know from your training and life experience." Then we asked, "Would you also be willing to open further to the Unknown, to invite Great Mystery to guide your lives and work as healers even more deeply?"

Each one of these remarkable human beings prayerfully considered going deeper in "partnership" with Spirit. Among those who immediately said yes to that invitation was a medical doctor named Sam. The workshop ended and he went home later that day and did a commitment ceremony to Spirit during his time of meditation and prayer.

Then he called us about a week later to share this remarkable story of healing:

He was making rounds at the hospital and looked in on one of his patients, a young man named Pete, who had been diagnosed with AIDS. Dr. Sam had tried almost every treatment he could think of and was feeling frustrated. Then he remembered his heart's desire to open to Great Mystery. He took a deep breath, inwardly prayed for his heart to open, and said, "Pete, I don't know what else to do. What does your wisdom say we should do?"

When's the last time your M.D. asked you that? Thankfully, it's beginning to happen more often.

Pete then demonstrated one of the greatest ways we all can open to Spirit. *He closed his eyes, took some deep breaths, paused a few moments, and reflected on the question.* Then he looked at his doctor and answered, "Will you hold me?"

Dr. Sam later told us he was keenly aware that the choice before him contained powerful healing possibilities, together with huge risks, both emotional and professional. Looking at his watch he thought, *I've got a lot of patients to see,* but he then made the choice that would change Pete's life and his own and ultimately change the way he practiced medicine. The physician climbed onto the bed with the young man and held him—for two hours! Dr. Sam said that as he held Pete, he too felt "held" by a tender, loving presence.

After two hours Pete's family arrived and Dr. Sam said to them, "Now you get to do this part." And that's what they did. For the next twelve hours, Pete's family took turns holding him. His father held him. His mother held him. Siblings and friends held him. Then, after twelve hours of this "ceremony," Pete died—healed! Was his body cured of

AIDS? No. Did he experience healing? Absolutely yes!

Over the next few weeks, Pete's family members called Dr. Sam to share stories of tremendous healing breakthroughs. After many years of anger, unforgiving attitudes, non-acceptance, and misunderstanding, the family was able to heal as they held Pete and one another in love. During twelve brief hours their attitudes shifted and only love remained. The Story of Love is the ultimate, sacred healing dream.

Holding the dream of healing in your heart helps to create healing and sometimes to cure. To be cured is to be relieved of the illness of body or mind. We've certainly seen many cures, remarkable and miraculous physical cures in which people create outcomes that defy medical prognoses. And we give thanks for these. To be healed is a far more sacred and bigger story than to be cured. Simply stated, though not so simply lived, healing is the soul's journey of conscious evolution, a story of waking up and remembering that we are eternal.

Sometimes, however, we resist the Story. In her book, *The Search for the Beloved*, Jean Houston writes: "... you may go to [Your Life] Story, kicking and screaming all the way and saying, 'I don't want to see! Please, I don't want to see!' This protest arrives when the thickening plot suggests a story that you do not like, that you find inconvenient, that seems devastating. Yet devastation, or at least radical surprise, is an inevitable and central theme of Great Story, which always engages us at our most fragile and wounded edges. Then, suddenly, in these events that wound, the ensuing holes make us holy, allow more information, more interchange, and more stories to come in."[10]

When the tide is low, people come from everywhere to

explore the uncovered rocks and tide pools, the beach treasures. When times are difficult, remember to look for the gifts that are uncovered by the "pounding surf." Some of the greatest spiritual experiences and revelations come in the bleakest times. This is true for many people whose stories I have heard in counseling and healing sessions. If it is true that we grow more profoundly and Holy Dream is revealed more fully during our hardest times, then perhaps we can ultimately give thanks for those experiences. We can even give thanks *during* those experiences by realizing that Spirit is at work revealing treasures and bringing us to our true selves.

When I, Margaret, was twenty-five, the love of my young life died in a car accident. This wasn't the first time I had "lost" someone dear to my heart. It was, however, a loss that truly shocked me. Life seemed to stop and I fell into the paralyzing grip of depression and grief. For many weeks I rarely talked with anyone and the few times I did, I could not hear the words of comfort.

People were most certainly praying for me because after many weeks of not leaving my apartment, I woke up one morning and felt compelled to go outside. The community where I lived was in an older, established part of town, with lots of beautiful parks, and I rode my ten-speed bicycle for several hours in and out of them. At the end of the day I rode into what I thought was yet another park. I was greeted by a sweet fragrance that filled the air and saw that freshly cut roses covered the sidewalk. I stopped my bike and stood, mesmerized, watching an ancient-looking woman wearing soiled leather gloves and a ragged straw hat, as she gracefully, carefully, pruned the roses. Colors fading and blooms drooping, they definitely needed to be pruned, and the perfume that filled the air was exquisite!

I approached the gardener woman and began, as we say in the South, "to chat" unceasingly. This was remarkable in itself because I had not felt like talking to anyone since the funeral. She just kept pruning the roses, glancing at me now and then, listening, nodding her head, but not saying a word. I told her that my Mom and Dad enjoyed gardening, though it was a lot of work; that I sometimes pulled weeds as part of my chores growing up; and weren't roses hard to grow, taking a lot of care; and maybe one day I would grow roses—and on and on and on.

Finally, I asked permission to gather up some of the cut roses and take them home with me. Without a moment's hesitation, she put her pruning shears aside and knelt down with me, carefully lifting the roses into my bicycle basket.

This ancient and wise "rose tender" then turned and looked deeply into my eyes and all the way into my soul. I heard her speak, but it was not in the usual way. Rather, her message was clearly impressed upon my mind and heart. She said, "Just as you still see the beauty of these roses, God still sees the beauty of your life, even though you have forgotten."

She didn't speak with her lips or make a sound. More importantly, her message touched my soul and impacted the path I would ultimately follow, one that would lead me into ministry, including counseling and facilitating healing with others whose journeys also contained heartbreak and loss. God is not confused. Everything in our lives is "recycled" and used for good—everything.

I got on my bicycle and rode out of the park. When I turned to wave goodbye, I read the sign on the gate: "St. Vincent's Convent—Keep Out." I later learned that some of the sisters there take the vow of silence. The voice of Spirit, however, was *not* silent. Was she my angel? Yes. Earthly or Heavenly? I don't know, and it doesn't matter. This experience, among others, led me to open more fully to the unseen realm, including the awareness that life and consciousness continue beyond the experience we call "death."

To this day, I can still remember the "ancient one" and the roses she gave to me. I filled every vase, every mayonnaise and jelly jar I could find! Petals dropped and colors continued to fade, though the fragrance lingered for weeks and seemed to be of "another world," crossing dimensional thresholds to remind me of the "many mansions" within and around us. I am sometimes aware of the scent of roses during healing sessions with individuals or groups. Some say it announces the presence of Mother Mary or Holy Spirit. I cannot prove any of this. I only know there is always a sense of peace and great love that comes with it, just like that blessed day years ago.

Every part of our journey holds sacred purpose. De Montaigne says it this way: "The things that matter most must not be at the mercy of [the] things that matter least." Seeing the things that matter most, deepening into the sacred insights of your stories and looking for how Holy Dream has unfolded, shifts the way you view the world and the way you view yourself. Eventually, Holy Dream leads you to *honor yourself and your place within the evolving consciousness of good in the world.* If that feels impossible right now, then at least consider that you are traveling on a path which has included pain and joy, hard times and easier times, and know (or imagine for now) that you are honored for simply saying yes. It is said that the angels are curious about what it is like to be human and that they are in awe of us for saying yes to this human journey.

Are you in awe of yourself, and your journey?

Ultimately, the most important story is how we see and interpret our lives. The story of how we feel and what we believe to be true about ourselves. St. Teresa of Avila, a 16th century Carmelite nun, implores us to know our inner magnificence when she writes in *Interior Castle*:

> The soul seems to me to be like a castle, made of a single diamond or of very clear crystal, in which there are many rooms, just as in heaven there are many mansions. It is a great shame not to know who we are in these terms. We become like a person who has no idea who he is, who his father and mother are, from what country he came. We seldom consider what it means to be created in the image and likeness of God, because all our interest is centered in the rough setting of the diamond and the outer wall of the castle; that is to say, in these bodies of ours. This castle contains many mansions, above, below, at each side; and in the center and midst of them all is the chief mansion where the most secret things pass between God and the soul."[11]

This "castle" is where Holy Dream resides, the Spirit of Creation, God, Holy Spirit. When we view life from this place, the Kingdom/Queendom of God within, precious anointing of Holy Dream guidance and awareness, flows between our soul and the eternal. Feelings of separateness fade along with the sense of being anything other than eternal. God-Self is a part of the evolving Holy Dream and

Holy Dream is the enlivening presence of God-Self.

The following ceremony invites honest and loving evaluation of the way you view yourself, your life, and your dreams. It also invites you to open your heart and allow healing to happen. With loving compassion, rather than judgment, witness and observe your thoughts and feelings. Be attentive, stay awake, and allow holy awareness and heavenly presence to hold, comfort, anoint, and renew you.

A Healing Ceremony of Self Re-Viewing

✧ As you prepare, give yourself the time and space to make this process a sacred ceremony. Go at a pace that is comfortable for you. If you choose, light a candle and put on soft music. Breathe deeply and steadily, consciously letting each breath center you in the present moment. Enter the experience with an open heart. Pause. Breathe. And reflect after each question. Allow your heart to respond with the answer that feels most healing and integral to who you truly are: an eternal spiritual being who is experiencing the human journey.

✧ Creatively design this ceremony in the way that works best for you. Take whatever time you need. It can be done in minutes or hours, days or weeks. Take one question and "live with it" for a period of time in your prayers, meditations, and reflections. Ask to receive wise counsel from your soul, God, Holy Spirit, or Divine Self. Call on the support of your angels, guides, your unseen circle, or the ancestors, and allow wisdom to come to you through dreams when you sleep or insights when you are awake. Write this wisdom in your journal. Go with Blessings into this ceremony.

✧ Are you willing to look for what's good and healing in your stories? Are you willing to look for Spirit, true purpose, and magnificence in your life's journey?

✧ What is the story you tell about yourself? In other words, how do you define yourself—by holy concepts or damaging definitions?

✧ How do you announce your circumstances to the world?

✧ If you did not have any damaging concepts of yourself, who would you be?

✧ How do you perceive others in your circle, your journey companions (those on the "good" list and those on the "other" list)?

✧ As Rumi the poet asks, "Who are you really? What is your real name?"

✧ Would you be willing to hold an immaculate concept of yourself? An inspired, spirit-filled, holy concept of yourself? If so, how does that look and feel?

✧ Are you willing to behold others in this way? How does this look and feel?

✧ In The Search for The Beloved, Jean Houston gives us this reminder: "You enter into the eternal place of the great patterns of creation and there get your codings, your dancing orders, to carry back onto the grid of time and space." What are your dancing orders?

✧ How is Holy Dream unfolding in and through your life?

IT'S NEVER TOO LATE TO BE BLESSED

Have you ever experienced the devastating effects of not being welcomed? How long have you held onto those feelings of hurt and disappointment? Maybe it still affects you to this day. Until recently, I felt the anguish of rejection from a trauma experienced at the age of nineteen. After over thirty years of praying and daring to dream that this feeling of rejection could be healed, a major shift took place, and I received one of the most profound healing experiences of my life.

In June 2000, Margaret and I were guest presenters at Unity Village near Kansas City, the national headquarters for the Association of Unity Churches. We offered our "Shifting Into Miracle Thinking" workshop that we present to churches all around the country. After our workshop, we felt really grateful that we were able to support many people and facilitate their powerful healing shifts, but little did I know that later that week it would be my turn to be healed.

The shift happened for me in another presenter's workshop entitled, "Coming Home," facilitated by a Unity minister, Sky St. John. Sky told us how he was trained to do the "Coming Home" workshop by Elizabeth Kubler-Ross. During his training, Elizabeth told a story that really touched Sky's heart, and when Sky retold the story, I felt a stirring in my own heart. Elizabeth's story went like this:

In one of her large workshop groups, which included a number of Vietnam veterans, she asked the vets to go and wait in another room so that she could speak privately to the remaining group. The vets agreed and left. She then told everyone else that a number of these men and women were not only dealing with grief, loss, and the devastating effects of war, but were also holding onto extreme feelings of not being appreciated or welcomed when they came back to America. Elizabeth declared, "We must begin to heal these deep-seated wounds because they're still affecting the vets to this day."

It was time to "re-do" the experience of coming home from Vietnam in a completely new, loving, healing, and supportive way. She asked the workshop attendees to represent a changed America, to shout out cheers when the vets came back into the room, as if they were coming home for the first time—to celebrate the vets in a loving, powerful way, to whisper tender, healing words, to fill them with encouragement, pride, and blessings. In other words, to welcome them home with gifts of love that would touch them to the very core of their being.

The group agreed to do this and Elizabeth invited the vets back into the room. As they arrived, the audience cheered and clapped, offering words of appreciation and blessings and lots of healing touch. Someone ran to the piano and began to play parade music. The energy was unbounded. Love, encouragement, and healing filled the room. The vets were so overcome with emotion that years and years of tears began to pour down their faces. They were overwhelmed with such powerful feelings that many of them fell to their knees, weeping. It was difficult for some to accept and contain this blessing, yet they were profoundly grateful to receive it.

Elizabeth directed everyone to create a circle around the veterans. Then she asked the vets to walk over to each person in the circle to receive a personal, individual welcome. She said, "You've come home and we welcome you."

The vets rose to sounds of heartfelt cheers, but some were so emotionally fragile that they began to tremble, could not support the weight of their emotions, and fell to the floor once again. Determined to continue, they crawled on their hands and knees around the circle, receiving many blessings and at last experienced the true homecoming they had dreamed of all those years. There wasn't a dry eye in the group. The vets weren't the only ones who received healing that day; everyone in the entire group was moved by this soul-stirring experience.

Sky related this magnificent story in his compassionate, gentle way and shared with us that hearing Elizabeth's story had opened his heart to the immense human need to feel welcomed. Everyone could sense the genuine emotion underlying Sky's desire to serve our group in this loving way. So, with much anticipation, we prepared ourselves to participate in our own "Coming Home" experience.

Sky asked if there were any situations in our lives where we did not feel acknowledged, honored, or supported, whether it was with our parents, other relationships, or a particular circumstance. He affirmed that in the Coming Home experience, we were being given an opportunity to transform old, unwelcoming energy into new blessings, to heal our wounds once and for all. As I thought about what Sky was saying, I realized that there is powerful healing medicine in being seen, recognized, and respected. When we are not seen and acknowledged, it affects our self-esteem, which in turn can prevent Holy Dream from being expressed through us. *If we don't feel welcomed, how can we welcome our dreams?*

I looked around the room to determine who might have had their dreams shattered by feeling unwelcomed. But then my thoughts shifted back to Sky when I heard him invite those of us who wanted to participate in the Coming Home healing blessing to gather in the back of the room. Everyone else was to go up front to be the "welcoming committee."

There must have been at least 150 people out of the 200 present that went to the front of the room to do the welcoming. Since I was a workshop presenter at this conference, I naturally started to walk toward the front of the room so I could support everyone else. Suddenly, I heard a still, small inner voice that spoke with crystal clarity saying, "David, go to the back of the room because there's something very important in your life that needs to be healed." The message was very powerful so I listened, trusted, and joined the others at the back of the room, even though at the time I wasn't clear what situation my inner voice was referring to.

I waited my turn as, one by one, each member of our group went up to the microphone and described the circumstances for which they needed healing. Each person was more than ready to "re-do" his/her situation in a powerful, loving way and experience the healing that was long overdue. The welcoming committee listened to many sad stories that began like this:

"My parents never told me . . ."
"My sister always saw . . ."
"My friends forgot . . ."
"My boss broke his promise . . ."

After speaking, each person started walking toward the front of the room. Everyone listened as Sky spoke two magical words into the microphone: "Welcome Home." (I interpreted that to mean coming home to Divine Self, the "true home," an opening of a closed heart.) Right on cue the welcome team cheered, applauded, opened their arms, and embraced each speaker with loving support and words of inspiration. Sky then said, "You have come home." Tears flowed freely as we all witnessed hearts opening and the miracle of healing.

As I watched this exceptionally emotional experience, I realized that my turn was getting close. Uncertain of what I would say, I still felt it was crucial for me to participate. Soon my turn came and as I walked up to the microphone, I was trembling. At the last second my inner voice spoke to me and said, "David, *YOU* were one of those Vietnam vets! For so many years you have been holding on to the pain of not feeling welcomed upon returning to America. It has hurt you for a long time and now is your chance to heal. Go For It! Tell your story." So I clutched the microphone and tearfully choked out the words, "I am one of those Vietnam veterans. My country and even my own father forgot about me while I was there, and when I returned, there was no one to welcome me home. This has hurt me for many years, and I've seen the pain in the faces of so many other vets over the years. It's time for healing, time for me to be healed."

A burst of applause rang out from the group. Everyone cheered and rushed towards me with open arms and practically knocked me down! Sky ran over to the piano and began playing patriotic parade music, starting with "God Bless America." The group touched my face and embraced me. They held me and whispered:

"Welcome Home . . ."
"We're so glad you're back safe and sound . . ."
"We missed you . . ."
"Thank you for being there for the rest of us . . ."
"Thank you for being here today for all of us . . ."

I was so overcome with emotion that I began to weep. Over thirty years of tears streamed down my cheeks, and I dropped to my knees. Time stood still. It was such a powerful feeling; I'll never forget it! After a few minutes, I managed to stand up and walk into the group. Everyone blessed me and held me with loving, life-affirming energy. Sky said, "You have come home, David. You are loved and we welcome you." This touched me to the core of my soul. Every cell of my body reacted to that experience.

As I walked through the group I was still shaking, but I could literally feel the pain leaving my body. The anvil of weight I had been carrying for so many years was lifting from my shoulders. The hurt was disappearing as I was held in the arms of love. I remembered that love is the healer. I felt the warmth of welcoming flow through me that I had wanted and needed so much from my country and my father. I chose to receive it and receive it I did! I could see the tears on some of the faces of the people blessing me, and I knew their love and support were real. It was the greatest healing I've ever received in my life, and my memory of it will never fade. My dream came true and I am so grateful!

Why did it come true? Because I never stopped praying and dreaming about the healing, I listened to my inner voice, the holy voice of Spirit, and took action. The voice of Spirit will always lead us in the holiest direction. It worked for me, and it will work for you, too.

Many people came up to me after the workshop and told me stories about their loved ones in Vietnam and the difficulties those loved ones faced when they returned home. These fathers, mothers, brothers, sisters, and spouses of Vietnam veterans also needed healing. They were grateful for my "Coming Home" experience because I also represented their loved ones who still needed to be recognized and appreciated by our country. These family members needed to welcome me as much as I needed to be welcomed! I never knew why I was in Vietnam until that very moment when I realized that everything really does happen for a reason. I can now use that experience for a holy purpose, and that purpose is to tell this story when I speak at church services, workshops, or conferences. My hope is that it will help Vietnam vets, their families, and others to remember that it is never too late to receive healing. No matter how much pain is being held inside, no matter what the circumstances are, it is never too late to heal the wounds and memories of the past.

Being welcomed home and telling my story has changed my life. If any of you feel unwelcome, pray and dare to dream for your blessing. Listen to the inner voice of Spirit and when the time is right, create your own version of the

Coming Home experience. Invite a support team to hear your story. Describe how you would like to be welcomed and allow your heart to open and receive. Healing those old wounds invites Holy Dream to unfold and manifest your heart's desires. Remember, it's never too late to be blessed!

I thank God. I thank the veterans. I thank Sky St. John and Elizabeth Kubler-Ross for their wondrous work that has been needed for so many years. God bless them. God bless all the veterans of all the wars. And God bless you. Dare to Dream. Why? Because Dreams Happen!

DARE TO DREAM PROCESS

David's "Coming Home" Meditation

This meditation is designed to help the reader experience the holy welcoming Presence of Spirit that lives so exquisitely in our hearts. Home is where the heart is. When we truly come home, the heart invites us to open to our Holy Dreams and fully receive all the blessings of the Divine.

If you'd like to read this meditation into a tape recorder and listen to it whenever you want, please do so. Otherwise, simply read it to yourself and allow the blessing of the heart to welcome you home.

✧ To begin, find a comfortable place to sit or lie down in a peaceful and relaxed manner. Take a deep breath and call forth the Divine Energy by saying the following invocation:

I call forth the infilling of the Divine Light of the Christ. (Or God, Beloved, Divine Mother, Holy Spirit, Buddha, Love, or Whatever Word best fits your image of Holy Presence.) I call forth a perfect circle of light and love to surround me. I call forth the holy healing breath of God to breathe within me. I call forth the power of the Holy Spirit to move through me now, to move the energy into my heart, to bathe my heart in love.

✧ Feel this loving energy filling your heart for a moment or so, and continue to breathe the holy breath.

I now call on the Holy Spirit to pour forth from my

heart like a river of healing light, touching each and every cell, renewing, restoring, and regenerating as it moves through me and around me in a halo of healing light.

✧ Pause for a moment and experience this blessing of Spirit flowing through you. Take note of how you are feeling and breathe.

✧ Now imagine you are going on a wonderful journey to a sacred place within your heart, a beautiful sanctuary called the garden of your heart. Picture yourself walking in your garden surrounded by all the exquisite beauty of nature. Vibrant plants and trees and multicolored flowers greet you on your path. It's a beautiful, sunny day, and everywhere you look there are magnificent angels all around you. The angels whisper blessings of welcome to you by saying, "You are never, ever alone on your journey, for we walk the path with you and love and support you every step of the way. May you be comforted in our presence."

✧ (Let yourself feel this blessing. Know the angels are with you.)

✧ As you walk on your sacred path, the angels cheer you on. All of nature embraces you. Soon you notice a beautiful glowing light that is approaching you on the path. As the light comes closer and closer, you realize this is the light of the Christ within your heart. The Christ walks up to you and looks into your eyes and says, "Beloved one, you have come home, and I am always with you in your precious heart. The Christ then reaches out with those powerful healing hands and touches your sweet, sweet heart, igniting it with exquisite healing energy that flows through you like a river of healing light, blessing each and every cell.

✧ Allow your heart to fully receive this blessing and know that love is the healer.

✧ Imagine the angels singing your praise as they did the day you were born. Listen to the blessings they are whispering to you. "You are so loved. Welcome home, dear one. The Christ loves you and welcomes you with open arms. You are not alone. There is no separation. The Christ is blessing you now and so are we. We are now wrapping our wings around you and holding you dearly to our hearts."

✧ Feel this holy presence embracing you and allow yourself the comfort of being held in love.

✧ Imagine that the Christ takes your hand and together you walk back along the path through the garden of your heart. Choose a flower from the garden that represents the holy presence living within you and place that flower upon your heart. Feel the peace your flower brings you. Take a deep God-breath. Know that you have come home. Home is where the heart is and God is home!

✧ Slowly find yourself coming back into the present moment feeling refreshed and renewed, filled with holy presence. Welcome Home!

SACRED
CEREMONY

Wildflowers are God's way of saying, "It's all sacred." Everything is an essential part of the whole. When my (Margaret's) parents, Grady and Lillian, were newlyweds in 1946, money was not available for "extras" like fancy flowers for their garden. So they dug up some wildflowers from a sandy-soil field in Florida and planted pink, purple, red, and white phlox in their flowerbed. A well-meaning neighbor saw what they had done, walked over and said, "You can't plant those phlox in your garden. They're wildflowers!"

Often our dreams are like wildflowers. They crop up at times or in places where we think "they're not supposed to be." Sometimes they don't "fit" with what we expect of ourselves or what others have expected of us. Dreams and inspired ideas can be lost if we do not honor their sacredness.

In his book, *Sins of the Spirit, Blessings of the Flesh,* Matthew Fox, former Catholic priest and founder of the University of Creation Spirituality, writes: "There is nothing wrong with the human species today except one thing: we have lost the sense of the sacred."[12] What if we viewed all of life and every moment as sacred? Would our lives and dreams unfold in a more meaningful manner? Spirit seizes us to see the sacred and do ceremony in the most unusual ways at the most interesting times.

This was the case for me on the Colorado River a few

years ago when I was "called" to perform a ceremony of "Learning to Trust." David and I were on another one of our famous canoe trips with thirty participants in fifteen canoes, shooting rapids. My partner and I had gone five days without tipping our canoe. Everybody else in the group had tipped, including David, and at the end of five days, I had a kind of smug "canoe-tipping" attitude. I did notice, however, that everyone else was having a whole lot more fun than my partner and I were—but at least we had not tipped!

I worked very hard to keep my canoe upright. Most of us do that—don't we?—with our financial canoes, our health canoes, our relationship canoes. Then, as much as we try to control life, something happens. Well, on the fifth and final day, the last hour of the trip and at the easiest, most calm part of the river, my partner and I paddled right over a submerged pillow rock. The canoe rolled over so smoothly it was like watching a scene filmed in slow motion. Nothing dramatic, but still scary as we slipped out of the canoe into the "drink."

We held onto the side of the overturned canoe and continued floating down the rapid. It was a hot July day and I thought, "This isn't so bad, the water actually feels great! Why was I so afraid of tipping over my canoe?" How many of us spend so much of our energy trying to keep from tipping? Then when it finally happens, we realize that our *fear* of tipping was a whole lot more frightening than the actual experience itself, and that we really are okay.

I looked downstream and saw that people were turning their canoes around and heading back in our direction. Help was on the way! I was relieved, and then suddenly felt inspired to look up. You see, I had been so busy keeping my canoe upright that I rarely took time to look anywhere but straight ahead. Much to my delight I saw two golden eagles circling above us. I'd never seen a golden eagle before! By now I felt really *glad* that my canoe had tipped!

Then my mind broadcast a "news flash." I remembered that earlier that morning the group packers had strapped and buckled the communal toilet into our canoe! Needless to say, I was driven to prayer: *Oh God! I sure hope that the toilet is strapped in, and buckled up really, really well.* As I prayed, hanging onto the side of that canoe, I realized how much that moment was like my life. *I'm not only floating down the river with my stuff,* I thought, *I'm floating down the river with everybody's stuff!* I'm sure some of you understand how it feels to carry other people's emotional baggage down the River of Life!

Holy Spirit seized my attention and "invited" me to see this event as an opportunity for sacred ceremony. The inner voice within my heart asked these important questions: Are you willing, Margaret, to let go of your human patterns of struggle, control, and fear? Are you willing to honor your ancestors, upon whose shoulders you stand, and at the same time release your life-depleting beliefs of doubt and difficulty? Are you willing to trust the universe and hold all life and all experience as sacred?

These are important questions that most of us would quickly answer, "Well, yes, of course." If so, then why are so many of us still holding on to struggle and the generational patterns that rob us of our joy? In that moment, in the water, hanging onto the side of the canoe with the "honey pot" strapped in right next to me, I performed a ceremony by saying, "I will no longer carry the generational patterns of shame, struggle, and fear. I say *yes* to releasing that which depletes my life energy and *yes* to trusting the Great River of Life." In that moment I said yes to living my life in joy, rather than just enduring it, and I had an epiphany, a knowledge that every soul with whom I was connected was also touched by my commitment. Whether our beloveds are living in the physical or the non-physical, every time we say yes to transforming the old generational struggles, every soul with whom we are connected is also blessed and renewed biologically, genetically, and energetically.

We're all connected. You *know* this! For many years as a theologian and spiritual teacher, I would say "We're all one, all connected." Then a few years ago I read a book on quantum physics, *In Search of Schrodinger's Cat*, by John Gribbin,[13] and I finally "got it" in every cell of my being: We really *are* all one, and all the souls with whom we're connected—our ancestors, our families, our children, and our communities—all those souls we hold in our hearts are restored along with us when we make a shift. You and I have a choice: we can either live in sacred energy or in scared energy. If we so choose, we can let go of the old human patterns of struggle and fear and open to the new patterns of thrival and living life in more sacred ways.

So, as I thought about all this, floating along, I made a choice to let go and live life with trust. As soon as I made that soul declaration, the other canoes reached us and we were rescued and brought to shore. Wet, muddy, and laughing, I walked up the embankment and was delighted to see a beautiful field of wildflowers. I knew that all was well. I recalled a Buddhist prayer that includes this thought: "Let us use this moment to leap beyond our fear, landing upright on Earth among the wildflowers."

Letting go and "landing upright" can be easy or not, simple or profound. The mystics talk about a process we sometimes go through when we give birth to an idea or dream. First, it's important to let go of old thoughts and patterns that no longer serve us, then we move into a time of preparation called the "threshold," which in turn leads to the birthing experience.

Some of us, it seems, have the hardest time in the middle part—the threshold. We like to move from what we know right to the next thing that we know, but we don't like to be in the middle part, which can also be called the "time of not knowing." Some cultures and spiritual traditions seek out this middle part as a time of Great Mystery, a profound place of rich healing possibilities. The mystics devote much discussion to the subject of entering into the mystery—the womb—where the preparation for birth happens. Sometimes we work very hard at not letting go, not allowing ourselves time in the threshold, which ultimately makes it very difficult to birth a new idea or form.

Ever see the little Angel cards from Findhorn? There is one called "Trust" that shows an angel who has just let go of one trapeze and is moving through the air towards the next trapeze so that she is presently hanging in mid-air. This is the middle part.

A great journey, however, happens in the middle part. And as we all know, we have to let go of one trapeze in order to gain the momentum to fly to the next trapeze. Sometimes, though, we keep holding on to that old trapeze, while simultaneously trying to cross the middle part and arrive at the next trapeze, the "birth," but it just isn't going to happen that way. The time of letting go and trusting, the time spent suspended in mid-air, can be the time when the deepest ceremony, the richest preparation, and the most fruitful inspiration happen. Letting go and trusting that the next "trapeze" will be there for you is all part of the sacred journey toward your dream.

A great teacher taught me that the entire journey is sacred, even if it's a very difficult journey. I call this teacher "St. Anthony." He began his life as a drug-addicted baby. The doctors said that he probably wouldn't live, but his grandmother asked the most important question, "If he were to live, what would it take?" The doctors told her that if he were to live, it would mean holding him virtually nonstop for the first two years of his life. Without hesitation, his grandmother said, "I can do that!"

His grandparents adopted him immediately. Anthony lived with them from birth to age six and flourished in a loving environment. Little did he know at his tender age of six there would be another drastic change when his grandparents both died within a few months of one another. This might have devastated some children, but not Anthony. He had received the gift of all-embracing love from his grandparents, as well as lots of support from a strong spiritual community of friends and surrogate family. All of this contributed to his amazing ability to adjust to his circumstances in a very spiritually advanced way.

Before they died, his grandparents expressed the hope that their other daughter, his mother's sister, would adopt Anthony. His future was uncertain though, because his aunt and uncle had made a decision not to have any children. Anthony, it seems, was an unexpected "wildflower in their garden." They decided to let him visit and then determine the best course of action.

As a part of the community of friends who supported his grandparents during their illnesses and transitions, I also developed a close relationship with Anthony. Because of this, I was privileged to make the trip with him to meet his potential new family, who lived far away in the Midwest. Our plane arrived late in Denver, so we had to run to catch our connecting flight, and, of course, it was the farthest gate away. I took Anthony by the hand, hoisted the carry-on bags over my shoulder, and we sprinted along the concourse. As we passed one of the ticket agents, I yodeled, "Call the gate and tell them to hold our plane! Please!" Of course, they didn't.

Anthony looked up at me with his great big smile and enthusiastically said, "Mawguet, are we having a wunning day?" I labored a rather tense grin and said, "Yes! That is exactly what we're having. A wunning day!" We arrived just in time to watch the plane back away from the gate. You know the feeling—fun, right? I was furious. But Anthony thought it was great to get to see the plane pull back from the gate and taxi out to the runway. "Wow, it's huge!" he said.

We marched—well, *I* marched—with great determination and Anthony skipped to the airline counter. I let the ticket agents know just how pleased I was about missing the flight. They rewarded us with two meal vouchers and the news that we had a five-hour layover. My first thought was: *Oh God! What am I going to do with a six-year-old in this airport for the next five hours?* I could only imagine that this was going to be an "interesting" experience.

Anthony grabbed the meal vouchers and thought this was just like winning the lottery! I was still fuming and

Anthony was delighted as we ate our "happy meals." Then we made our way to a mostly empty lounge area where we still had more than four hours to wait for the plane. I was not looking forward to this, and I forgot the first rule in seeing the Sacred unfold in all of life's experiences: Ask, "What is God up to in this experience?"

Anthony was unaffected by the wait and proceeded to unload his backpack, pulling out his Power Rangers, trail mix, coloring books, and crayons. He then made a large circle with all of these "sacred elements," stretched out on his belly in the middle of the space, and began to color. I thought to myself, "This will last for about ten minutes." But in fact, this sacred ceremony lasted until we were called to board our plane.

Across the hallway in another waiting area, a little boy began to cry. It was the kind of wail that no matter what the parents did, there was no consoling him. Anthony stood up, looked at the boy, and with great determination beckoned for the boy to come over. His parents watched as the little boy, still wailing, walked timidly across the hallway, and stood at the edge of the circle. Anthony looked inquisitively at the boy and pointedly asked, "Don't you have any coloring books?" Sniffling, the boy answered "No." Surprised, Anthony said "Well!" and tore a page from his coloring book, slid it across the circle along with a few crayons, and motioned for the little boy to come into the circle. It's interesting to note that the boy did not enter the Sacred Circle until he was invited. Anthony then asked him, "How old are you anyway?" Wiping tears with his sleeve, the little boy sniffled, "Three." Anthony looked up at me, rolled his eyes, and said, "Figures!"

As the hours easily passed, other children found their way to Anthony's circle, each one standing on the edge until they were invited to enter. The circle kept growing, the edges expanding to make room for them. Parents gradually gathered around the circle to witness this scene with amazement. Forgotten were the books we were reading and the frustration over missed connections. Our planes were late, but we were "propelled" into another kind of flight: to the eternal sacred moment where time does not exist, but where love, peace, and what truly matters does. We all experienced *this* sacred journey together.

I realized that I would never have these sacred hours with six-year-old Anthony again, and that this was a rare opportunity to be present with the Beloved. So, I took it all in and received the blessing that the Divine was presenting to me through Anthony. I felt so grateful that I was part of this sacred ceremony.

If you do not yet feel your entire journey is sacred, would you be willing to consider that it *could* be? What if every experience is meant for instruction, insight, and celebration of who you truly are? St. Anthony helped me know that this is true. I am happy to report to you that Anthony's aunt and uncle, who never wanted children but who were willing to consider the idea, now feel their lives are far more complete with Anthony. He is emotionally, physically, mentally, and spiritually thriving!

So, this is what I learned: Always carry crayons, coloring books, trail mix, and Power Rangers in your backpack! Seriously, that's a good idea. And always, always, always be open to the sacred in every moment, especially those moments that appear to be difficult. And always create sacred ceremony wherever you go. Everything that we experience, no matter what it looks like, holds sacred purpose. Why not make each step of the journey a conscious one? What if all of life is like Anthony's sacred circle: experiences that "come round" to give us their blessings and truth? What if all of life is a Ceremony, a Journey of Sacred Moments and receiving blessings!

The Sacred Ceremony of Receiving

Learning how to receive blessings when they come your way is extremely important in manifesting your dreams. Ponder these questions: Do you consider yourself to be a great giver—one who gives freely of their time, talent, or treasures? Most of the people in our workshops fit nicely into this category. We work with lots of "givers and caretakers."

The next question is, Do you consider yourself to be a great receiver, one who easily accepts gifts, blessings, and acknowledgments? Very few people we work with consider themselves to be great receivers. How about you? Many of us were taught that it is better to give than to receive. Sound familiar? Some of us still have unresolved issues about worthiness, self-esteem, and deservedness that keep us from being fully able to receive.

Now, consider this: Do you think there is a correlation between difficulty in receiving and not being able to fully manifest our dreams? One of the most important ingredients in bringing forth our dreams is the ability to receive. If we're closed down because we don't feel we deserve the blessings, then we're not functioning from the heart. The heart functions through absolute love and respect for self and knows without a shadow of a doubt that we *all* deserve *all* of God's Blessings.

Sacred Ceremony can be very effective in helping us open all our channels to living in our heart and gratefully, gracefully, receiving God's gifts without hesitation. Do you remember what you were taught to say as a child when given a gift? "Thank you." Those magical words are very important and when said sincerely, they indicate that you are open, ready, willing to receive the blessing, and are grateful for it.

We teach a powerful sacred ceremony in our workshops to help people feel close to each other and to open their hearts to receive blessings. We would like to teach it to you. We recommend that you practice your version of this experience with family members, including children, at work, in schools, or in any group where you want to build trust, offer encouragement, and create an atmosphere in which inspiration can flow.

The ceremony is called "The God Seat" or "The Thank You Seat."

- ✧ Bring together a group of three or four people and have them sit in a triangle or circle, facing each other. If you are working with a larger group of people, create as many small groups of three or four as necessary.

- ✧ One person sits in "The God Seat," facing the other two or three people who are the angels. The person sitting in the God seat stays fully present with the angels and receives their blessings in the form of compliments, words of encouragement, and inspiration. After receiving these blessings, all the God-seat person may say is "Thank you." Now, we realize that some of you may want to explain how you got to be so wonderful, or you might try to negate the loving words being spoken to you, so remember, all you can say is "Thank you" and receive the blessings!

✧ If you feel uncomfortable while receiving the blessings, simply breathe the holy breath into your heart and ease those feelings with love.

✧ The angels' job is to give encouraging, heart-to-heart words to the person in the God seat. If there is any difficulty in thinking what to say as an angel, then breathe into your heart and say what you, yourself, would most want to hear.

✧ The angels take turns, giving compliments one at a time, and continue to go back and forth for several minutes until the person receiving is feeling blessed.

✧ Remember to breathe during the experience. Breathing is a very good thing to do on this planet!

✧ Each person in the group gets a turn to be in the God seat and to be an angel.

✧ After the entire experience is over, have everyone in the small group describe to each other how it felt to receive blessings in the God seat and how it felt to give blessings as an angel. Was one part easier than the other was? This is the time to share special insights and thoughts about one's ability to give and receive.

The practice of giving and receiving blessings is a wonderful ceremony we can do to keep our hearts open. This, in turn, makes it so much easier to manifest our dreams because we are creating them from a sacred place within us that is open and receptive. God has more blessings for you than you could ever imagine! So, give yourself this gift: Let go of the beliefs or patterns that keep you closed and depleted of life energy, then open your heart and say *yes* to the gifts and allow them to pour in. Receive them with gratitude in your heart and say the two magical words: "Thank you." That keeps blessings, including inspiration for your dreams, flowing your way in a never-ending Sacred Ceremony.

CREATING AND LIVING YOUR DREAM

Creating and living a dream begins with the very first thought of the dream, and then continues in a creative step-by-step process to the eventual manifestation and incorporation of that dream into your life. Writing this book, for example, was a very interesting process that began after the events of September 11, 2001. Like many others at that time, we increased our prayers of peace for our own hearts as well as for the world. During this time of prayer, we received profound inspiration to write this book. We shared the inspiration with each other, discussed the idea, prayed about it, and each of us got the green light when we heard our own inner voice, saying, "Go For It!" We knew this was an important step for both of us personally and for the people we work with. We felt so much enthusiasm and joy in our hearts that we said a resounding *yes* to Spirit and began the visioning process.

We contacted family and friends, both near and far, and asked them to be holy visionaries for our dream. We also invited a group of friends from our home community to meet with us, to listen to our dream, and to give us their support and encouragement as our vision team. We clearly stated this vision to everyone present: "We will be inspired, creative, faithful, and disciplined to write a well-received book that will increase hope, create healing, and support people to live their holy dreams." The vision also included a timeline for completion and for the financial resources for editing and publishing. Then we all prayed together and held this holy vision in our hearts. Everyone agreed to continually hold the vision and to give us supportive encouragement until completion of the book.

During the writing process, we experienced the most amazing serendipity, things coming together at the perfect time in perfect ways such as ideas, prosperity, editors, book designers, and heartfelt support. We also got to experience some testing of our faith, some bumps in the road such as feeling tired or stuck, thinking that it was impossible to complete the book in our timeframe, and the frustration of losing hours of work due to a computer glitch. During these times, we had many opportunities to call on Spirit, as well as our vision team, to help us stay on course, increase our faith, and keep believing that our dream was possible. With each breakthrough or accomplishment, no matter how large or small, we gave thanks, which is an important ceremony to keep the energy flowing for the creation of a dream.

We would like to offer some tips to help you create and live your dream. You can use them as a guide to supplement the creative ideas you already have. As you dare to dream, remember to make the entire process a sacred journey, to move forward confidently in the direction of your dream, and to Go For It.

Identify Your Dream — Establish a clear vision of your dream in your heart through prayer, meditation, or reflection. Feel the energy of your dream. Does it lift your spirit and fill you with enthusiasm and hope? Welcome your dream into your heart as you would welcome a guest into your home, or as you would celebrate the birth of a child.

Years ago, we met a Swahili woman who worked as a delivery room nurse and she told us that in her country when a child is born, the community gathers and sings a ceremonial song of welcome to the child. The message of the song is that a place has been reserved for this child under their communal tree, a place belonging exclusively to this child whose arrival has been long awaited.

Make a special place in your heart just for your dream and then celebrate it. Listen to how it speaks to you and guides the process of its own creation. Look for and be open to receive supportive energy and information about your dream such as insights, inspired ideas, sleeping dreams, chance conversations, and other synchronicities. Remember, what you see is what you get.

Do you believe your dream is possible? Greater possibility thinking contributes greatly to the creation of your dream. The image you hold in your heart is of vital importance because that image is the map or blueprint that your heart and mind will follow.

Vision Team — Call family, friends, and colleagues who you know will be fully supportive of you and your dream. They will be your very own "dream team." Clearly state your vision to them. Include details like resources needed and timeframes. Your vision also serves as your affirmation so it needs to be positively and faithfully stated. Let the team know what kind of support you want from them. Then, be open to receive encouragement, supportive energy, creative ideas, and suggestions, all of which can be a wealth of added inspiration for you. During the process of creating your dream, know that you can always call on your vision team to be of support whenever you need it.

Action Steps and Homework — Take action and do whatever it takes to move forward in your dream. This includes doing whatever homework is necessary—such as assessing your present resources and evaluating your life experience, training, and skills. Then, determine what additional resources are needed, for instance, finances, schooling, research, or consultation. Continually cheer yourself on by repeating positive, uplifting statements and affirmations, such as, "I'm doing a great job," or "Everything is working together for the good of my dream." Periodically look in the mirror and give yourself a "two thumbs up!"

Do Good Things for Yourself — It is always important to take really good care of yourself, but it becomes especially important when you are creating and living your dream. When we nurture ourselves, we are highly motivated to move forward in our dreams. Remember to eat nutritious food, exercise regularly, enjoy nature, pray and meditate, and surround yourself with uplifting people. Get plenty of rest and take time to celebrate your Sabbath. Pursue whatever renews you, such as having a massage, attending the theatre, dancing, reading, listening to music, developing creative projects, or spending time with loved ones.

Keep the Faith When There are "Bumps in the Road" — If you have any bumps in the road, any challenges or difficulties during the creation of your dream, don't panic. Instead, pray, meditate, and call upon your vision team to help you regain inner focus so that you are able to move forward again in your dream process. Challenges are often coded messages that can revise, redirect, and re-energize your dream in powerful ways.

One of the ways we deal with bumps in the road is to embrace them with loving energy by reciting the 23rd Psalm. That affords us an opportunity to learn from our difficulties and helps us to remember that we are not alone in creating our dream. It is very comforting to know that God—Divine Mind—is with us every step of the way.

The following is our metaphysical interpretation of the 23rd Psalm. To us, "The Lord" is the Sacred Perspective or God-Consciousness that guides us all.

The Lord is my shepherd; I shall not want.
He maketh me to lie down in green pastures.
Healing, regenerative blessings for body, mind, and emotions.
He leadeth me beside the still waters.
Renewing and restoring my faith and giving me peace.
He restoreth my soul.
Helping me to remember my true nature as an eternal spiritual being who has the help and support of Spirit.
He leadeth me in the paths of righteousness for his name's sake.
Right thinking, clear decisions, seeing all that needs to be done for creating the holiest dreams.

Yea, though I walk through the valley of the shadow of death, I will fear no evil

Struggles, challenges, and fears, forgetting my magnificence and my connection with Holy Spirit.

For thou art with me; thy rod and thy staff, they comfort me.

The power and presence of God is with me, and all is well.

Thou preparest a table before me in the presence of mine enemies.

Working with Spirit, I face my greatest fears and overcome them.

Thou anointest my head with oil; my cup runneth over.

I have the blessing of Spirit and an overflowing abundance of inspiration, creativity, courage, strength, stamina, and resources to follow my heart's wisdom and create my dream.

Surely goodness and mercy shall follow me all the days of my life: and I will dwell in the house of the Lord forever.

Spirit is within me and supports me. The evidence of my partnership with Spirit is everywhere I look in my life. Blessings abound.

The Re-Do Process for Clearing Blocks — Most of us have had experiences in our life that have caused distress, and sometimes that distress has created blocked or "stuck" energy. If this feels true for you, then that energy might still exist within your cellular memory. If so, a clearing of that energy is necessary in order to move forward in the creation and realization of your dreams. One of the ways you can clear these blockages is to create a "re-do" of the original experience that caused you distress. By imagining that same scene happening in a more empowering and successful way, you can heal the old feelings from the original experience. You can also release the blocked energy and see that event as a learning experience and a "building block" that positively influences your dream. (Refer to Dare to Dream Process at the end of this chapter.)

Margaret's sister, Pam, offers a great bit of wisdom for stressful times: "It's only a movie!" she says. We all know what happens on a film set. The camera rolls, Take One is announced, the director says, "Action," the actors act, and then the director says, "Cut." Sometimes it's necessary to shoot the scene again, which is called Take Two. When this happens, changes are made and things are done differently, perhaps better lighting, an additional camera angle, changes in dialogue, or actors given a new hand prop or a different emotional interpretation.

The subconscious doesn't distinguish between past, present, and future events. Everything is happening in the eternal moment of Now. Because of that, you can re-do past scenes. The mind and heart will work in unison as the director to help release the cellular memory of old wounds that are stuck in the emotions and the body.

Margaret's life was greatly impacted when she decided to heal her feelings about a traumatic experience that she had involving public speaking. This is her story:

"From a very early age, I always knew that I wanted to be a teacher. Unfortunately, I was afraid to speak in public, which happens to be a common fear. Throughout high school I worked on overcoming this fear, and by the time I got to college, I was doing better. However, in my freshman speech class, I had a major setback.

During my presentation on the life and work of the poet, Rod McKuen, I wanted to illustrate his writing style by playing a particular poem on one of his 33 rpm records. Much to my embarrassment, I couldn't find the right groove into which to place the needle! The more I tried, the more flustered I became. My hands were shaking and sweat poured down my face. I dragged the needle across the record, scratching it, then completely lost my train of thought and all concentration. I tried to recuperate and finish my speech, but by that time I was so frustrated that I couldn't speak. I just wanted to get out of the room but couldn't because in order to receive my grade for the class, I had to stay for the evaluation! I looked to the professor for some kind of help, and unbelievably she added more fuel to the fire by torching me with the words, "Miss Allen, don't ever become a public speaker!" I was stunned, and all I remembered after that was the class laughing at me. I had to work very hard to hold back the tears.

I carried feelings of embarrassment and inadequacy about this event until my sophomore year when I was writing an outline for another talk that I was scheduled to give in my history class. Suddenly I "stumbled upon the idea" of re-doing my disastrous speech class experience. I imagined that I was back in that speech class and saw myself calm, poised, speaking eloquently, and easily "finding my groove" as well as finding the groove on the record. I saw myself successfully finishing the speech, then looking out at the audience who were smiling and giving me a standing ovation. Then the professor lit my fire by saying, "Margaret, what a fantastic speech! You're a magnificent public speaker!" As I imagined hearing these words, I was completely uplifted and my feelings of inadequacy transformed.

By the time I finished preparing for my history class speech, I felt confident and at ease. Before I actually entered the auditorium, I mentally pictured the entire speech flowing smoothly and being a complete success. During my presentation, I projected my voice with great confidence so as to be heard by everyone in the room. I was definitely channeling my "future self," who knew how to speak in public with ease. The re-do practice paid off and my speech was a huge success. My classmates applauded and cheered. My professor smiled at me, shook my hand, and enthusiastically said, "Congratulations, you're a great public speaker!" Later that semester, the healing was complete when I received an evaluation from my classmates as having the "most professional delivery" out of all ninety students in the class. I continued to practice my public speaking and since 1981 have traveled throughout the world making my living as a teacher and professional public speaker."

Give Thanks — Every day, focus on what you have to be grateful for and freely give thanks to all those who support you, including God and your dream team. Periodically make a gratitude list of all the blessings in your life. Review your list as often as you need to, particularly when there is a bump in the road, as this will help keep your spirit uplifted and keep you on course with your dream. Staying in gratefulness increases the life force energy of the heart and draws your dream to you.

Trust that God is at Work in Your Dream — Every day, remind yourself that God is on your dream team and is working with you. Remember, you are never alone in the process. Call on God to help you remember that all things are possible, and know that God's dream for you is to experience life to the fullest, to be happy, to learn from your experiences, to love and be loved, and to live your dream.

DARE TO DREAM PROCESS

Thirty-Day Coaching Plan to Create and Live Your Dream

Choose the dream that you want to manifest and practice the following thirty-day, step-by-step coaching plan. Immerse yourself fully in your dream. Live it! Become an active, integral part of it. Empower yourself and believe in your ability to create it. This plan is meant to be a guideline. Use it exactly as it is, or modify it to meet your own personal needs.

✧ **Step 1, Days 1 - 7**

Meditate and pray for a crystal-clear vision of your dream. When you receive that vision, pray on it everyday in your meditations—seeing, feeling, and understanding it. Listen to your heart's guidance about the dream. Call on divine support to uplift and inspire you. Keep a journal of insights about your dream. Draw or paint it. Dance it. Breathe life into it!

Know that you are never alone in this process. Trust that God is always with you and on your dream team. Remember, God is your greatest cheerleader.

✧ **Step 2, Days 8 - 14**

Call family, friends, and colleagues who you know will be fully supportive of you and your dream. Tell them briefly what you want to create and ask them to be on your vision team. Invite them to come to your home as a group. Do a centering prayer, and then clearly state the vision of your dream. Tell your team how they can be of support to you. Have the team pray together and hold the holy vision with you for your dream. Then receive their words of encouragement and support. Let them know that their ongoing support is very important and ask permission to call them for encouragement whenever necessary. Also, let your team know that it will be very helpful for you to receive phone calls, E-mails, or any other kind of "Go For It!" messages from them.

Take any and all necessary action steps, including giving thanks, to keep your dream moving forward. Remember, the Navajo give thanks for the rain before they ever see the first rain drop. So, it is important for you to give thanks and celebrate your dream even before it is fully manifested. Take good care of yourself. Eat nutritious food. Exercise regularly. Do your spiritual practice consistently. You are, after all, the holy vehicle through which your dream is being born.

✧ Step 3, Days 15 - 21

Keep the faith. Great dreams take time to manifest. If there are bumps in the road, don't worry. Center yourself through prayer and meditation. Call on your vision team for support. Do what it takes to maintain or regain your focus, which could include reciting the 23rd Psalm.

If you determine that your bump in the road is related to a stressful event in your life which is now keeping you from moving forward in the creation of your dream, then this would be a good time for a re-do.

Begin the re-do process by reflecting on the event that you experienced as emotionally difficult. Breathe a holy breath into your heart and bless this memory.

Now, see yourself transforming this scene to a whole new experience. Create a more supportive, uplifting, and successful experience by imagining yourself as confident, empowered, and centered in your truth. See all the other "players" in this scene cheering you on with genuine support and encouragement. Make the outcome as brilliant, creative, and powerful as you can. You're the Director!

✧ Step 4, Days 22 - 28

Continue to pray and meditate on your dream. Know that all things are possible. Keep your faith and enthusiasm strong by celebrating with a "Giving Thanks Ceremony." Thank God first. Then make a list of all that you have accomplished so far. Invite your team over to celebrate the progress you are making toward realizing your dream. Update your team on any changes or revisions so they can continue to hold a clear vision with you. Give thanks for all of their support and encouragement. Break bread together.

✧ Step 5, Days 29 & 30

The last two days are a time to evaluate the effectiveness of this coaching plan. Determine what has worked for you, what you want to modify, and how you want to continue. Make this a sacred process of listening to Spirit and your own heart wisdom.

If you feel that this thirty-day plan has been helpful, then include the elements that worked for you in the creation of your next new plan. In this way, you can continue the process of manifesting and living your dream.

God's greatest desire is for you to be abundantly blessed. So, believe in yourself as God believes in you. Dare to Dream. And remember, *YOU* are God's Dream come true.

REFERENCES

1. Paul Pearsall, *Making Miracles* (New York: Prentice Hall Press), 1991

2. Alan Cohen, *I Had It All the Time: When Self-Improvement Gives Way to Ecstasy* (Des Moines, WA: Alan Cohen Publications), 1995

3. Wayne Muller, *How, Then, Shall We Live? Four Simple Questions That Reveal the Beauty and Meaning of Our Lives* (New York: Bantam Books), 1996

4. Robert Francis, "Summons," *Robert Francis Collected Poems 1936 - 1976* (Amherst, MA: University of Massachusetts Press), 1976

5. Key Carey, *The Third Millennium* (San Francisco, CA: Harper San Francisco), 1995

6. Hyemeyohosts Storm, *Seven Arrows* (New York: Harper & Row), 1972

7. John Beeson, *Plea for the Indians* (Fairfield, WA: Galleon Press), 1982

8. Deepok Chopra, *The Way of the Wizard: Twenty Spiritual Lessons in Creating the Life You Want* (New York: Harmony Books), 1995

9. Jeanne Achterberg, *Woman as Healer* (Boston, MA: Shambala Publications), 1990

10. Jean Houston, *The Search for the Beloved: Journeys in Mythology and Sacred Psychology* (New York: JP Tarcher/Putnam), 1987

11. St. Teresa of Avila, *Interior Castle* (Garden City, NY: Doubleday), 1972

12. Matthew Fox, *Sins of the Spirit, Blessings of the Flesh: Lessons for Transforming Evil in Soul and Society* (New York: Harmony Books: Hardback), 1999

13. John Gribbin, *In Search of Schrodinger's Cat: Quantum Physics and Reality* (New York: Bantum Doubleday Bell Publications), 1984

PRODUCT DESCRIPTIONS

***Dare to Dream*, Book:** .... $14 each

✧ Dare to Dream is a sacred journey of creating Holy Dreams for self, family, country, and the world. It encourages the shift from survival dreams to thrival dreams; the healing of old beliefs that hinder creativity; and the rekindling of hope to know that all things are possible. This book inspires us to "Go for It and Live Our Dreams!"

Teaching Cassettes: .... $10 each

✧ *David's Meditation of the Healing Heart* (Side A) — Beautiful healing meditation that many people use in their healing process, including cancer treatments and surgery.

David's Guardian Angel Meditation (Side B) — Meditation to meet your guardian angels.

✧ *Shifting Into Miracle Thinking* — A healing meditation by David; Stories and Inspiring teachings by Margaret on the subjects of healing, miracles, and gaining God-perspective.

✧ *The Power of Healing in Forgiveness* — Forgiveness Meditation by Margaret; Stories and powerful teachings by Margaret about opening the heart and creating a sacred space for healing through the power of genuine forgiveness.

✧ *Finding the Divine in Human Relationships* (Side A) — Meditation by David; Teachings by Margaret on the subject of seeing the Divine in all of our relationships.

Leap of Faith, Moving Mountains & Creating Miracles (Side B) — Meditation by David; Teachings by Margaret on the subjects of moving through fear, increasing faith, and creating remarkable outcomes of healing and transformation.

✧ *Dare to Dream* — Meditation by David; Inspired stories about dreaming the Holiest Dreams, including David's "Vietnam Healing Story" and Margaret's "Don't Quit" Story.

✧ **Shift Happens T-Shirts:** . . . .$20 each
White, 100% pre-shrunk cotton, sizes Large or Extra Large
Front: "Shift Happens" in purple lettering with Starburst Logo
Back: "Shifting Into Miracle Thinking" in purple lettering with Starburst Logo

✧ ***Dare to Dream* T-Shirts:** . . . . $23 each
White, 100% pre-shrunk cotton, sizes Large or Extra Large
Front: "Dare to Dream" in purple lettering with beautiful, multicolored *Dare to Dream* book cover Image.

Both T-Shirts are shown on our website:
http://home.mindspring.com/~miracles1

PRODUCT ORDER FORM

Name:_____

Address:_____

City:_____ State:_____ Zip:_____

Phone:_____ E-Mail:_____

Visa/M.C.#:_____ Exp. Date:_____

Signature:_____

Send Check, Money Order or Credit Card information to:
Margaret and David Hiller,
238 N. Wightman St., Ashland, Oregon, 97520
Inquiries: miracles1@mindspring.com

Quantity:_____ *Dare to Dream* @ $14/book $_____

Quantity:_____ *David's Healing Meditation* @ $10/cassette $_____

Quantity:_____ *Shifting Into Miracle Thinking* @ $10/cassette $_____

Quantity:_____ *Power of Healing in Forgiveness* @ $10/cassette $_____

Quantity:_____ *Finding the Divine and Leap of Faith*
         @ $10/cassette $_____

Quantity:_____ *Dare to Dream* @ $10/cassette $_____

Quantity:_____ *Large Shift Happens T-Shirt* @ $20/shirt $_____

Quantity:_____ *Extra Large Shift Happens T-Shirt* @ $20/shirt $_____

Quantity:_____ *Large Dare to Dream T-Shirt* @ $23/shirt $_____

Quantity:_____ *Extra Large Dare to Dream T-Shirt* @ $23/shirt $_____

E-Mail Your Inquiries about Special Discount Rates for Bulk Order.
Please allow 7 – 10 days for delivery.

Shipping and Handling
For Orders:
$20 or less $3.00
$21 - $40 .... $5.00
$41 - $60 .... $7.00
$61 - $100 .... $9.00
$101 - $200 .....$12.00

Sub Total $_____

S&H $_____

TOTAL $_____

PRODUCT ORDER FORM

Name: _____

Address: _____

City: _____ State: _____ Zip: _____

Phone: _____ E-Mail: _____

Visa/M.C.#: _____ Exp. Date: _____

Signature: _____

Send Check, Money Order or Credit Card information to:
Margaret and David Hiller,
238 N. Wightman St., Ashland, Oregon, 97520
Inquiries: miracles1@mindspring.com

Quantity: _____ *Dare to Dream* @ $14/book $_____

Quantity: _____ *David's Healing Meditation* @ $10/cassette $_____

Quantity: _____ *Shifting Into Miracle Thinking* @ $10/cassette $_____

Quantity: _____ *Power of Healing in Forgiveness* @ $10/cassette $_____

Quantity: _____ *Finding the Divine and Leap of Faith*
@ $10/cassette $_____

Quantity: _____ *Dare to Dream* @ $10/cassette $_____

Quantity: _____ *Large Shift Happens T-Shirt* @ $20/shirt $_____

Quantity: _____ *Extra Large Shift Happens T-Shirt* @ $20/shirt $_____

Quantity: _____ *Large Dare to Dream T-Shirt* @ $23/shirt $_____

Quantity: _____ *Extra Large Dare to Dream T-Shirt* @ $23/shirt $_____

E-Mail Your Inquiries about Special Discount Rates for Bulk Order.
Please allow 7 – 10 days for delivery.

Shipping and Handling
For Orders:
$20 or less $3.00
$21 - $40 .... $5.00
$41 - $60 .... $7.00
$61 - $100 .... $9.00
$101 - $200 ..... $12.00

Sub Total $_____

S&H $_____

TOTAL $_____